# ESCOFFIER

by Marjory Bartlett Sanger

BILLY BARTRAM AND HIS GREEN WORLD

ESCOFFIER

# *Escoffier*

## MASTER CHEF

★ ★ ★ ★

## *Marjory Bartlett Sanger*

FARRAR STRAUS GIROUX
NEW YORK

Copyright © 1976 by Marjory Bartlett Sanger
All rights reserved
First printing, 1976
Printed in the United States of America
Published simultaneously in Canada
by McGraw-Hill Ryerson Ltd.
Library of Congress Cataloging in Publication Data
Sanger, Marjory Bartlett.
Escoffier, master chef.
Bibliography: p.
Includes index.
1. Escoffier, Auguste, 1846–1935—Juvenile
literature. [1. Escoffier, Auguste, 1846–1935.
2. Cooks. 3. Cookery, French] I. Title.
TX649.E8S26 1976    641.5′092′4 [B] [92] 76–14810
ISBN 0-374-32227-9

# To Dilly

## Cailles glacées Maryland

"Prepare the quails as for an *entrée* and poach them for twelve minutes in a strong veal stock, with Champagne. This done, put them each into a small, oval mould; fill up these moulds with cooking-liquor, cleared of all grease and strained, and leave them to set on ice.

Now prepare a *Granité* [sherbet] with pineapple juice.

Set this *Granité* in a pyramid on a dish inserted in cracked ice. Turn out the quails and place them round the *Granité*; fill up the gaps between them with small heaps of pitted cherries, *poached* in syrup for a few minutes and quite cold.

These dishes wherein a sweetened preparation and a *glazed* one are introduced together are highly esteemed in summer; but they really belong in the culinary repertory of hot countries."

Georges Auguste Escoffier
*Le Guide Culinaire*

# ACKNOWLEDGMENTS

*"They'll not get it all in a book, I think,*
*Though they write it carefully."*

This observation of Ezra Pound's in *The Goodly Fere* reflects the experience of almost every writer. To those who enabled me to get as much as I could into this book, I should like to offer my gratitude and appreciation.

Dean Robert A. Beck, of the School of Hotel Administration at Cornell University, was most generous in lending material. My thanks also go to Katharine Kendall Brewster, Charlotte Moughton Brunoehler, Renata de Jara, Professor John B. Hamilton, Henry Powell Hopkins, Alice Anderson Hufstader, Helen Currie Martin, and the Alliance Française de Rollins College.

# CONTENTS

# ESCOFFIER

# WHERE THE TRUFFLE WAXES

*"She is happiest in places where the grapevine grows,
where orange trees send out their perfume, where the
truffle waxes and wild game and fruits may flourish."*
                    *Brillat-Savarin to* Gasterea

We are accustomed to thinking of nine muses: *Gasterea,* sometimes called *Nectambrosia,* the muse who presides over the pleasures of taste, has been ordained the tenth.

Why a tenth muse? Art, music, and dance attract us; we are educated by history, challenged by astronomy, amused by comedy or touched by tragedy, and enhanced by poetry, whether epic or lyric. Our souls are undoubtedly sustained by the offerings of the nine classic muses.

What about our bodies? That ephemeral cord which "keeps body and soul together" has many names: health, nourishment, diet, dining . . . essentially food.

"Think this over carefully," wrote Pierre-Charles Monselet, a Nantes gourmet, over a hundred years ago. "The most charming hours of our life are all connected, by a more or less tangible hyphen, with a memory of the table."

One hardly needs an excuse to write about food. Or about that most blessed individual, the cook. Nature creates the seed, man harvests the crop, but it is the cook who presides not only over the stove but also at dinnertime over our five senses (yes, even hearing), and thereby controls our well-being and, presumably, a portion of our joy.

"Good cooking is the basis of true happiness," wrote Georges Auguste Escoffier in French across the portrait photograph which now hangs in the house where he was born.

No one ever understood better the marriage of *cuisine* and *bonheur,* or practiced the art more honestly, more inventively, or more superbly.

He changed the dining habits of nations; he cooked for queens and emperors. Yet his motto remained: *"Faites Simple."* It was with these two words that he changed his world.

Once, on the Irrawaddy River, I met an English woman who asked the title of my new book. When I told her, she said, "Good. That's my favorite steak sauce."

And I had to smile, thinking on the one hand of the great chef's determination that a sauce should fit the entrée like a lady's tight skirt, and on the other of his gratification in pleasing women, whoever and wherever.

A second familiar reaction is: "Oh, yes; that's a famous restaurant, isn't it?" Doubtless there are many Escoffier restaurants. I was not inspired to do special research on this subject. But I did dine one memorable evening at the Escoffier in Copenhagen, which a guidebook recommended as serving "meals as French as a meal can be outside France."

Another guide designated it the only restaurant in Scandinavia where one may order the same dinner "in two sizes—large if you're hungry, small if you're not."

The master would have approved of both these commendations.

In any case, to prove that the man was neither a sauce nor an eating place has not been the purpose of this book. To introduce a brilliant chef and some of his creations to an audience increasingly interested in food and its preparation was the original concept. "Gastronomy adds joy to all situations and all ages."

The inclusion of some of the history of the classic French cuisine was natural and necessary. And the presentation of a serene, imaginative, and altogether delightful person was the inevitable result.

One day, looking through an index, I came across Escoffier's name sandwiched between *"Escargots"* and

"Eskimo Pie." And I thought how somehow fitting that was to his unique combination of elegance and simplicity, and that no other chef in the world would have been more amused or content.

Marjory Bartlett Sanger

# 1

★ ★ ★ ★

# THE RENAISSANCE
# OF THE ART

*"Since the renaissance of the art, I have been constantly
employed at dinners and festivities."*
*Antonin Carême*

When Caterina de' Medici set sail from Florence to
Marseilles to become the bride of Henry, Duke of
Orleans and second son of King Francis I of France,
she smuggled aboard the galleons a couple of her
cooks. She had overheard her ladies-in-waiting gossip-
ing in the *palazza* about the inferiority of French cuisine and the fact that the chefs did not understand the
preparation of sweets, particularly *gelati,* her favorite
water ices.

Although only fourteen, Caterina, an orphan and
the last legitimate descendant of Lorenzo the Magnificent, was accustomed to having her way. She even
dared confess the smuggling to her uncle, Pope Clement VII, who was to perform the marriage ceremony.
The Medici Pope magnanimously forgave without in-

forming the child that the King of France himself had specified the dowry include Tuscan *cuoci* and their recipes. A Renaissance man at heart, Francis after several forays into Italy had become only too well aware of the culinary shortcomings of his native land and the need for Italians in the court kitchens.

Caterina and her fiancé had never met. The betrothal was arranged to strengthen relations between the two countries, a customary procedure in those days. Henry, only one month older than Catherine, as she was now to be known, was visibly unhappy with the arrangement. He barely spoke to his bride during the week-long nuptial festivities, a rebuff which Catherine excused as shyness. But the King rejoiced in the delectable *dolci* of the wedding feast, and the Pope presented his niece with seven of the world's most magnificent matched pearls, because, as he prophesied, in spite of the presence of the Dauphin, Henry's older brother, one day his Caterina would wear them as Queen of France.

The year was 1533. A year later Pope Clement would be dead, from eating poisonous mushrooms, it was rumored. And fourteen years later Catherine would indeed be Queen. Three years after her marriage, the Dauphin had died, as her uncle had foreseen, so that when Francis I died in 1547, Catherine's husband became King Henry II of France.

The great Medici fortune, part of which Catherine brought to the French court, had been enhanced in past centuries by the spice trade, in which the family had extensive financial interests. During its long rivalry with Venice, which since the days of the Crusades had been a powerful sea-republic, Florence struggled to share the Mediterranean trading rights.

Propitiously situated at the head of the Adriatic, Venice had the advantage. Crusaders returning there from the Holy Land introduced a taste for spice, and stimulated a demand. Salt, pepper, saffron, ginger, nutmeg, and cloves found their way to the tables of the Doges. When Pope Innocent threatened excommunication to those who dealt with the Saracens, he was forced to relent. By the middle of the fifteenth century, Venice was importing twenty-five thousand tons of pepper and ginger alone every year.

It is often suggested that spices were primarily used to disguise the taste of spoiled food. This might have been the case on long sea voyages, but the idea hardly pertains to the glittering society of the "Pearl of the Adriatic." The inclusion of spice in the cuisine of the nobles lent a new and exotic quality. In his *Grand Dictionnaire de Cuisine,* Alexandre Dumas wrote that "intellectual faculties seem to have soared in an enduring exaltation under the influences of spices."

Florence, which has been called the heart and soul of the Renaissance, would have what Venice had. Controlling the economy, the Medicis invested heavily in the spice trade, and grew even richer on it. It was in the family's blood to be fond of good food; in 1469 Lorenzo the Magnificent celebrated his marriage with a series of feasts that lasted for three days.

Historians have stated that the bloodiest wars in the world were fought for spices, and kingdoms rose and fell thereby. Certainly more territory seems to have been acquired, and more trade routes attempted, for spices than for gold. Kings and queens sent their fleets to far-off and uncharted lands; admirals and merchants risked their lives and fortunes.

One queen, Isabella of Castille, dispatched a Genoese to the Indian Spice Islands to find her a share of the treasure. On his second voyage, in 1493, Columbus brought back a new kind of pepper from Hispaniola, a red variety that achieved great popularity.

A few years after that, Vasco da Gama sailed around the Cape of Good Hope and across the Indian Ocean to Malabar and Calicut, exulting, some say, "For Christ and spices!" With Portugal then controlling the coasts of both Africa and India, as well as the sea routes along the way, Italy had first to share with the Portuguese its long domination of the spice trade, and then to abandon it altogether. It was the best thing that could have happened to Italian cookery.

No longer able to rely on a multitude of spices to transform, alter, or enhance, the *cuoci* were forced to become inventive in their preparations. For the first time in centuries, food began to taste like itself rather than like the highly seasoned sauces which enveloped it. Inventiveness gave way to naturalness; Italian cookery, of necessity, found the quality that for many years the court of "Catherine, the Florentine" would be praised for. It turned out to be the foundation of France's *haute cuisine.*

While her husband dallied with Diane de Poitiers at Chenonceau, Catherine, Queen of France, presented sumptuous *fêtes à l'Italienne* at Fontainebleau, Chaumont, Les Tournelles, and Amboise, where her parents had been married a year before her birth.

Catherine was half-French, extravagant by nature, and above all a true product of the Renaissance. Manyfaceted, creative, witty, exuberant, controlled, and self-assured, at least on the surface, she directed her *cuoci* to prepare feasts that opened and dazzled Parisian eyes.

What had these eyes been accustomed to seeing? What was on the menu at the court of France during the reign of Francis I?

Game, for one thing. Francis was an expert hunter, and there were always wild animals, both feathered and furred, hanging from the kitchen eaves. Butcher's meat was considered "too ordinary," but one menu called for "66 chickens cooked as grouse," also three young bustards and thirty-three ibises.

Peacocks were particularly spectacular when they

arrived at the banquet table dressed in their plumage
. . . shades of ancient Rome!* Swans also appeared in
their plumage *(revêtus de leur plumes)*. Actually, in the
early sixteenth century, French cooking was not unlike
that of northern Europe, with highly seasoned and
spiced meats, usually boiled and masked with thick
gravy. There were root vegetables, mostly turnips;
fruit was offered for medicinal purposes. And among
the wealthy, "pyramids" were popular.

A "pyramid" consisted of a large platter upon which
was piled a variety of meats: suckling pigs, haunches of
mutton, loins of veal, wild turkeys (an exciting import
from the New World, brought from Mexico by
Cortés), capons stuffed with damson plums, pen-fat-
tened guinea hens, and ducks. Sometimes a hundred
birds would appear. These were put together with a
variety of sausages and eggs, nuts, vegetables, and
fruits (usually not eaten); and the whole array was
proudly borne into the dining hall, sometimes to top-
ple and fall apart before reaching the table.

Such disasters did not deter chefs from vying with
one another to create grander and more unusual struc-
tures. And hosts adopted this means of indicating the
extent of their wealth and hospitality, particularly if
royalty was being entertained. It is depressing to imag-

*Many of the dishes mentioned only briefly in the text are de-
scribed in more detail in the last section of this book, "Treats and
Receipts" (page 171).

ine how many of these "pyramids" King Francis must have had to confront.

Another popular conceit of the period was the "animated pie." The recipe for this comes from a sixteenth-century cookbook called *Epulario, or, the Italian Banquet,* and describes how "To make Pies that Birds may be alive in them, and flie out when it is cut up . . . which is to delight and pleasure shew to the company." They seem to have been a particular "delight and pleasure" at wedding feasts "to pass away the time," according to *The Accomplisht Cook, or the Art and Mystery of Cookery,* whose author, Robert May, offers an ingenious variation of his own: that of replacing the birds with snakes, which, he adds in an endearing understatement, "will seem strange to the beholders which cut up the pie at the table."

Whether Catherine had an "animated pie" at her wedding feast, we do not know for sure, but it is on record that her confectioners created differently shaped ices for every day of the celebration, and that the guests pleaded, and offered bribes, for the rules of making such wonderful objects—but to no avail.

In all fairness it must be admitted that banquet conceits and elaborate culinary displays were neither exclusively Italian nor especially French. Richard II's chefs created marzipan portraits of banquet guests. The very year that Catherine married Henry of France, Henry of England took Anne Boleyn as his second bride. At *their* wedding feast, the first course alone consisted of twenty-eight dishes, "besides subtleties and ships made of wax marvellous to behold."

In addition to her ices, Catherine brought to the kitchens and tables of her new country: olive oil, oranges, sugar, artichokes (which she loved in omelets), broccoli, beans (the Florentines' beloved *fagioli*), and the tiny new peas, *piselli novelli,* which the French were quick to adopt as their own and which we know today as *petits pois.*

During the Middle Ages, the Saracens had introduced rice from the Orient; the child Caterina had been served *risotto* with nearly every meal. Crusaders brought spinach, which they planted along the Arno; *ova affrittellate alla Medici* was a popular spinach omelet. It was largely because of the prominence of the Medici and their addiction to foods and feasts that Florence came to lead the rest of Italy in culinary excellence.

When the King's doctor forbade him to eat the spinach Catherine's chefs grew and prepared, it is reported that he cried: "What! I am King of France and I cannot eat spinach!" Today the word "Florentine" on a menu usually means that the dish contains spinach in some form.

The pasta that Catherine brought to the court was not well received, but her truffles were, and they sent Frenchmen crying: *"Peila! Pei-la!"* and *"Vas y cherche!"* training their pigs and dogs to root under every oak tree.

*Pintade à la Médicis* is still listed in some cookbooks; so are artichokes Catherine de Médicis. Catherine also suggested the grilling of *carpa,* the goldfish-like inhabitants of her father-in-law's ponds at Fontainebleau. These had been described centuries before in Rome as "delicate, expensive fish eaten by princes."

She encouraged the taste for songbirds, particularly larks and thrushes fattened in cages; sweetbreads, a delicacy of the Renaissance; *salsicci,* herb-scented sausages; *zabaglione;* and frangipane cream. "The court of Catherine de Médicis was a veritable earthly paradise," one observer wrote.

The Florentines, during their celebrated rebirth, had not been engrossed simply with the exalted arts of painting, sculpture, and architecture. Swept along by the high tide of creativity, inspiration and achievement also found their way to the kitchen. The most sophisticated cuisine the Western world had known began to emerge.

There is a saying that a well-nourished race produces geniuses. Dating from Etruscan times, Tuscan *cucina* was one of the oldest and best in Europe. Blessed by fertile farm and grazing land, silver-green olive groves, and hillsides of vineyards, Tuscan cooking was, and still is, literally drenched in olive oil and wine.

Interest in gastronomy flourished equally among the diners and the cooks. New dishes were demanded, and then invented to fill the demand. It was in their sauces that the Italian *cuoci* were at their most inventive. Every cook was a sauce chef; he had to be, since he might be called upon to prepare a certain entrée from start to finish.

In France, with perhaps only one or two *sauciers* to a royal kitchen, dishes were bound to be somewhat monotonous. Worse than that, the sauces were so thick and opaque that often the food itself, both its taste and its appearance, was hidden as behind a domino.

On the other hand, the keynotes of Florentine cooking had always been simplicity, care, and restraint. Unlike some sections of Italy, the *cucina* of Tuscany has a classic emphasis on the excellence of its raw materials and the perfection of their preparation. And it is this *cucina* that became the basis of the French cuisine practiced through the subsequent centuries by the greatest chefs in the world.

The first time that Catherine de Médicis saw the château of Chenonceau arching across the river Cher, she was on a hunting expedition with her father-in-law. Seeing that she was moved by its loveliness, Francis promised it to her upon his death. "When I am gone, it shall be yours," he said. This was not to be. On his ascent to the throne, Henry presented the château to the only woman he loved, Diane de Poitiers.

Upon *his* death, Catherine wasted no time in removing Diane from Chenonceau, and soon began there a series of magnificent banquets, fancy-dress parties, pageants, and balls. "Naval battles and water fêtes on the Cher were followed by fireworks and torchlight dances in the long galleries, while spirited encounters took place in the woods and gardens between troops of gentlemen and ladies of the court disguised as satyrs and nymphs."

At the reception his mother gave at Chenonceau to celebrate his coronation, Henry III appeared "dressed as a woman, jewels in his hair, earrings, pearls around his bare neck . . ."

At her fêtes would also appear some of her own favorite Italian delights: *tortini di carciofi*, little tarts of baby artichokes sautéed in olive oil with eggs; *risotto; piselli novelli alla Fiorentina*, those small peas cooked in olive oil and chervil; and of course *fagioli all'uccelletto*, white beans seasoned "like little birds" with sage, garlic, and pepper.

These might be followed by an imposing array of sweets: ices, flowery and fruity flavors in elaborate shapes; and marzipan heraldry or coats of arms involving crowns and eagles, dragons, unicorns, lions, and other such beasts. Sometimes these edible sculptures rested on beds of spun sugar wreathed with almonds and vine leaves. The court cuisine had come a long way since "four-and-twenty blackbirds baked in a pie."

Less than one hundred years after Catherine's wedding, another Medici married a Henry, King of France. This was Maria, granddaughter of Cosimo,

Grand Duke of Tuscany, from the "younger" branch of the family that had also produced Pope Clement. Henry IV had been ruler of France since 1589, the very year Catherine died. Marie, as she came to be known, arrived from Italy in 1600 to give Henry the heir that his former wife, Marguerite de Valois, was unable to do. Like her distant cousin, Marie did not come empty-handed.

With the realization that her husband needed a son, Marie was advised to bring along love-inducing beans; she brought them in a wine bottle.

*Fagioli nel fiasco* is an ancient Tuscan dish: white beans marinated and cooked in olive oil, garlic, and sage, inside a chianti flask over smoldering charcoal. Our word "fiasco" obviously derives from what occurs if the bottle breaks during the cooking.

At Marie's wedding feast, one table "appeared covered with flowers, with fountains at each end and an infinity of little birds which flew around the room."

Henry IV, also known as Henry the Great and *Le Grand Béarnais,* was charming, outgoing, and popular, unlike Catherine's Henry. Like him, he was inattentive to his wife. Nevertheless, they had six children. History discloses that he often devoured several hundred oysters at one sitting. But he is also rumored to have munched on cloves of garlic.

In Italy, the aromatic herb basil was the symbol of love; more than that, it "maketh a man merrie and glad." Francis I had tasted it at the banquets of Andrea

Doria in Genoa in the form of *pesto genovese,* a savory mixture of fresh basil, olive oil, garlic, grated Parmesan, and *pignolia.* Even before Marie hopefully imported it, *pesto* had crossed the border into Provence, where, as *pistou,* it became the principal ingredient of a fragrant vegetable soup.

It was Marie's realistic and agriculturally minded husband who desired a *poule-au-pot* for every household, declaring that "there would not be a peasant so poor in all my realm who would not have a chicken in his pot every Sunday." Those of us who believed that "a chicken in every pot" was an original political slogan of the Depression days know better now.

It remained for one more Italian, the imaginative and enterprising Francisco Procopio dei Coltelli, to open the first café in Paris, which still exists on the rue de l'Ancienne-Comédie. To it he brought pastries and cakes, and the delicate water ices whose recipes Catherine's *cuoci* had guarded like state secrets or crown jewels. Procopio added cream, and turned his "ice cream" into an instant success. That first ice-cream parlor, now called Le Procope, became the favorite café of Voltaire, and was visited by Napoleon, Robespierre, Balzac, Victor Hugo, and Benjamin Franklin, and by Talleyrand when his chef, Carême, was not supervising his kitchens. Liqueurs, an Italian institution popular with the Medici queens, were also featured at Le Procope.

In 1643, a year after Marie died in exile, her grand-son became King Louis XIV of France. During his long reign (a great part of it spent in dining) *haute cuisine,* and also *la cuisine bourgeoise* and *la cuisine regionale,* attained high peaks. This was partly because of a man named François Pierre de La Varenne who, in 1651, published a cookbook called *Le Vray Cuisinier François.* It was a timely assessment and explanation of the evolution of Franco-Italian cooking.

La Varenne said he had learned to cook from the Florentines in Henry IV's kitchens, but in a way his recipes were even more imaginative than the Italians'. *Ecuyer de Cuisine* of the Marquis d'Uxelles, La Varenne disapproved of heavy masking sauces for meat, preferring to bring out its natural flavor with pan juices or drippings, mixed with lemon or vinegar, and thickened when necessary with a roux or egg yolks. His best-known contribution was later named for his master, the Marquis. *Sauce duxelles* is a concentrated hash of mushrooms, shallots, and onions, finely minced, seasoned, and simmered in butter and oil until almost black.

To fighting men in the field he also sent dishes: turkeys stuffed with raspberries, and boned, roasted chickens in bottles sealed with corks of pastry. The instructions to the troops read that after reheating the bottom of the bottle should be cut away with a diamond!

"Eating well," declared one historian of the time, "was a preoccupation with all who could afford it." It therefore became essential among the nobility to hire a superb chef. Louis XIV's own steward, the Marquis de Béchamel, made his contributions, the most famous being the classic white sauce that bears his name.

But the simplicity that La Varenne endorsed was yet to be attained. At the marriage of his daughter at Versailles, the "Sun King" offered his guests courses which contained one hundred and sixty dishes each. Like Henry IV, Louis himself thought nothing of devouring one hundred oysters at a sitting. It was during his reign that *pot-à-oie* became famous. A goose would be stuffed with sausage, foie gras, truffles, and "aromatic herbs." When it was served, "the most refined persons ate only the stuffing; they left the goose for the servants, yokels, and the poor."

Then there was the celebrated instance of Vatel, *chef de cuisine* of the Prince de Condé, who in 1671 had invited the King and an entourage of several hundred for a spring hunting weekend at Chantilly Castle. The moon was full, the tables were set up in the daffodil garden, and fresh fish from local streams were on the menu. When the fish failed to arrive, Vatel stabbed himself three times. "His death," wrote Mme de Sévigné, "spoiled the party."

And so the renaissance of the art of the new cuisine was eventually accomplished. The Medicis had made their mark. The French court was relying on its chefs for resplendent repasts; noblemen and peasants alike were reaping the rewards of culinary expertise because descriptive cookbooks, available to all, were beginning to be published.

It remained for someone to sort out of the abundance and the enthusiasm that accompany any rebirth a set of logical and practical rules. That "someone" emerged in the person of a young Frenchman with the unlikely first name of Marie-Antoine. In any case, Antonin Carême, as he came to be known, is described as the "Escoffier of the Regency."

# 2

★ ★ ★ ★

# CARÊME:
# THE CLASSIC CUISINE

*"The destiny of nations depends on how they nourish themselves."*
*Jean Anthelme Brillat-Savarin*

It was while Carême was working as an apprentice in the patisserie of a M. Bailly in the rue Viviénne in Paris that an important customer visited the pastry shop. Charles Maurice de Talleyrand-Périgord, a minister in Napoleon's Consulate, had been placed in charge of arrangements for a banquet celebrating the Peace of Amiens in 1802. Talleyrand, a self-styled gourmet who once claimed that giving fine meals was one of the two essentials of life, declared that only M. Bailly should design the *pièces montées.*

Bailly designed, but the "subtleties" in cake, biscuit, almond paste, and spun sugar for the table of Napoleon were actually prepared by the young chief pastry cook. "I used my drawings and my nights in his service, and he repaid me with kindness," Carême said in his memoirs. "It was with him in his establishment that I became an inventor."

Talleyrand was sufficiently impressed with Carême's inventions to hire him as his personal chef. "I left M. Bailly with tears in my eyes," Carême went on. "I had learned to execute every trick of my trade, and made unique, extraordinary pieces by myself . . . I left the pastry shops behind altogether, and devoted myself to preparing great dinners. It was enough to do."

Carême remained with Talleyrand for twelve years, furnishing his table, as he said, "at once with grandeur and wisdom." Neither man felt the need for false modesty; they suited one another well. Together they worked out the menus. Carême acknowledged that his employer's expenditures were "both great and wise at the same time."

Each recognized the diplomatic value of the grand repast. On the eve of the Congress of Vienna, Talleyrand informed Louis XVIII: "Sire, I have more need of casseroles than of written instructions."

"During the prodigality of the Directoire," wrote Alexandre Dumas in *Le Grand Dictionnaire de Cuisine*, "Carême refined cooking into the delicate luxury and exquisite sensuality of the Empire."

Carême met Laguipière, chef of Napoleon, who urged him to improvise. "From behind my stoves," Carême announced, "I contemplated the cuisines of India, China, Egypt, Greece, Turkey, Italy, Germany, and Switzerland. I felt the unworthy methods of routine crumble under my blows."

But he did not forget his early training at the patisserie. "The Fine Arts are five in number," he wrote and was quoted by Anatole France, "to wit: Painting, Music, Sculpture, Poetry, and Architecture—whereof the principal branch is confectionary." In proof of this he spent days studying and sketching the buildings of Paris, and poring over engravings in the Bibliothèque Nationale. He made meticulous architectural drawings for his set-pieces: his fish aspics, poultry galantines, and baskets of fruit, as well as his elaborate structural desserts, for which he was a veritable carpenter in sugar. That these creations, these fantasies in food, were seldom touched did not distress him. His ideal, he said, was "to present *sumptuously* the culinary marvels with which I enriched the tables of kings."

A familiar "culinary marvel" still served today is the charlotte russe, beloved of children, that concoction of ladyfingers and Bavarian and whipped creams. At a banquet for twelve hundred in the Grand Gallerie of the Louvre in 1815, Carême invented and presented to the reinstated Bourbon royalty in the person of Louis XVIII a dessert he wanted to call *charlotte parisienne,* but which achieved fame first as *charlotte Malakoff* and then as charlotte russe. In Russia it is known as *charlottka.*

"I sent them," Carême wrote in *Le Patissier Royale,*

"all ready to serve along with the orders for pastry sweets which were placed with me by the great houses."

In the meantime, a great house of another sort was being constructed across the English Channel. At a fishing village, mentioned in the Domesday Book as Bristelmestune, George Augustus Frederick, Prince of Wales and Prince Regent under George III, had designed a many-minareted gold-and-white pleasure dome of fantastic proportions and influences, mostly Moorish, Indian, and Chinese.

"Prinny," as he was called by some, paid his first visit to Brighton in 1783, the year before Carême was born. The Prince was twenty-one and interested in a Dr. Richard Russell's reports of the medicinal benefits of sea bathing. Already overweight and overindulgent (he confessed to being "rather too fond of women and wine") and also with a tendency toward gout, Prinny found the salt waters indeed beneficial. And so began an unexpected and unprecedented period of splendor for the small town (which Thackeray once called "kind, cheerful, merry 'Doctor' Brighton") as the regal entourage moved in, and, under the supervision of John Nash, the building of the Royal Pavillion began on the spot where fishing nets used to be dried.

Of all the state apartments, the Banqueting Room was the most magnificent. From a ceiling depicting "an

Eastern sky partially obscured by the broad and branching foliage of a luxuriant and fruited plantain tree" hung a crystal-and-copper "gasolier" thirty feet high and weighing nearly a ton, ornamented with lotuses, water lilies, and dolphins. Dragons and "magical birds" were also involved.

"Of the enchanting effect when fully illumined . . . it is scarcely possible to conceive," reads a justifiably enthusiastic account of the time. "In mid air, a diamond blaze . . . an artificial day."

That the menus hardly lived up to the "enchanting effect" was a source of some pain to Prinny. Thick white sauces, sometimes with mushrooms, sometimes with hard-cooked eggs (recipes from John Farley's *London Art of Cookery*) became popular the first year the Prince visited Brighton; they continued to subdue fish and fowl. "One ate the sauce without looking too carefully beneath it," reported Carême later.

The Prince Regent was well aware that the glories of the Regency did not extend to its kitchens. What was to be done?

News of banquets *à la française* had crossed the Channel. The French Revolution put a temporary end to their resplendence, although Louis had munched on roast chicken during his trial, and dined on six cutlets in his cell after his condemnation.

But as the Napoleonic Era emerged, so did a revived interest in fine cuisine. Napoleon himself, in spite of Laguipière and many others, is said to have gulped his meals in an un-gourmetlike fashion. He ate irregularly and untidily, demanding large amounts of food at the slightest twinge of hunger. Once, endeavoring to impress some guests, he did attempt an omelet, which, flipped from the pan, ended on the floor.

English noblemen, innately suspicious of anything foreign, particularly viands, were traveling abroad and returning with an incipient appreciation of Continental cooking, although some are reported to have lamented a lack of boiled leg of pork, pease pudding, and bubble-and-squeak. William Hazlitt called French cuisine an "abomination," and recommended that any Englishman confronted with it "get near enough the door to make his exit suddenly."

In 1808, however, a literary gourmet who is credited with reviving the interest in fine food after the revolution published a book called *Le Manuel des Amphitryons.* In his work, Grimod de la Reynière (his name was a pseudonym) laid down rules not only for chefs but also advice for hosts as well. Such as: "A host who does not understand how to carve is like the owner of a fine library who does not know how to read."

Indefatigably, he designated the quantity and proper succession of courses, according to the occasion and the number of guests. "Thirteen is dangerous at the dinner table only when there is just enough to eat for twelve." The more guests, the more courses; and no plate must appear to be empty. "The host whose guest is obliged to ask for anything is a dishonoured man," he declared. "The great point is to eat hot, nicely, and a great deal."

"He gave us the best dinner I have ever eaten," maintained Alexandre Dumas. La Reynière believed that five hours was "a reasonable latitude for a . . . refined meal," and deplored the use of leftovers. "A warmed-over dinner is worthless," he asserted.

As to how to handle the help: "Allow them to steal," he advised philosophically. "It was ever so."

Potatoes from Britain, tomatoes, songbirds, and sausages from Italy, and curry from India were all popular in France. Rice, almonds, and vine leaves came from the Near East. Interest in new ingredients, as well as the new dishes concocted from them, ran high. With the basis of the old pre-revolutionary opulence already laid, and the elegance of the Directoire acknowledged, the scene was set for the emergence of *la cuisine classique.* Chief exponent of this appeared to be the handsome and self-assured young man who called himself Antonin Carême.

It seemed entirely natural that the Prince Regent should want him for his chef. Thus was made the ultimate concession to the superiority of French cooking.

The fall of the Empire had left Carême temporarily

stranded. Talleyrand had resigned, declaring that, deprived of heat and water, he would consume nothing
but glazed cold meats and well-chilled wines. So that
now when a call came from Brighton, Carême, doubtless with many misgivings about leaving France, nevertheless responded.

It is ironic that the five hundred and fifty copper
utensils in the *batterie de cuisine* in the Great Kitchen of
the Royal Pavillion came from Apsley House, the London home of Sir Arthur Wellesley, First Duke of Wel-
lington and vanquisher of Napoleon. Gastronomic history records, however, that the Duke was no more a
gourmet than Bonaparte.

Carême served as chef for Prinny for parts of 1816
and 1817. In his *Journal* of the time, J. W. Croker
described the kitchens and larders: ". . . such contriv-
ances for roasting, boiling, baking, stewing, frying,
steaming and heating; hot plates, hot closets, hot air
and hot hearths, with all manner of cocks for hot water
and cold water, and warm water and steam, and twenty
saucepans all ticketed and labelled, placed up to their
necks in a vapour bath."

There were also various Doulton stoneware barrels
for beer, cider, vinegar, and other liquids, a huge flour
bin, and an "imposing" clock. Columns of gilded cast-
iron tubes branching forth into copper leaves carried
out the pseudo-Oriental theme of the rest of the Pavillion. The Prince is reported to have enjoyed dining in

the kitchen now and then with his servants. At least the food was hotter.

On the wall today is a handwritten menu of a banquet prepared by Carême for *"Le Prince Regent, Servie au pavillon de Brighton, Angleterre, 15 Janvier 1817. Menu de 36 entrées."* One hundred and sixteen dishes are listed, beginning with a selection of soups including a pink purée of pearl barley and carrots *Crécy.* "I have seen kings and emperors at table a thousand times, and all ate *potage* with relish," Carême announced.

The fish courses were followed by "larks in individual patty cases of oven-toasted bread lined with a creamed chicken-liver mixture; boned, stuffed partridges in aspic; and truffled fillets of hazel-grouse." Then came "a ring of fillets cut from the breasts of young wild rabbits," and a round of veal *à la royale* "enrobed in sauce and extravagantly garnished."

Of course, there would have to be the set-pieces, "spectaculars built of lobster, turkey, and ham"; edible, ornamental, and above all meticulously architectural depictions in pastry and cake of the Pavillion itself which Carême, an architect at heart, had called, at first glimpse, astounding.

There is no doubt that in composing his menus Carême made concessions to the British taste in food, but, as one historian has said, "he made them with the greatest *panache.*"

"You will kill me with a surfeit of food," the Prince

is said by his chef to have protested. "I have a fancy for everything you put before me." To which Carême says he replied: "Your Highness, my great concern is to stimulate your appetite. It is no concern of mine to curb it."

One of Carême's lasting innovations was initiated while in England and named for the Prince: *garni à la régence.* It began with his concept of decorating or trimming a fish dish with other seafood; that is, with similar textures and flavors. Whereas the often incongruous contrasts of the "pyramid" had been a mélange of fish, fowl, and red meat, *régence* garnishes were designed to harmonize with what they embellished.

Shellfish decorated with fish quenelles, fish with shrimp or lobster, poultry with chicken quenelles and mushrooms, sweetbreads with foie gras and truffles were important contributions of Carême to that unique blossoming of British culture called Regency.

Traditionally *garni à la régence* implies quenelles ornamented with truffles, sautéed sliced foie gras, cockscombs, mushrooms, and thick ovals of truffle in a *velouté* sauce.

After a while, Carême began to miss "that most, most alluring French conversation." He also found it difficult to educate and elevate English taste in food. The fogs rolling in from the Channel depressed him, as did the atmosphere of London, which he found "too sad an abiding place for a man whose soul, out of kitchen hours, was given to study."

For he longed to write as well as cook. He had already published *Le Patissier Royal Parisien* in 1815 before going to England. It was filled with indignation. He was irritated that "gloomy" cookbooks were being produced by unqualified chefs "lacking in taste, full of witless remarks and wild promises that if instructions were followed, fame would quickly follow after."

"I have revenged the Science," he thundered, pointing out that the only way to achieve success was through "strenuous and dedicated effort." He constantly dreaded dying before completing his writings. When the Baron Rothschild (for whom he worked seven years, thus making . his table "the best in Europe") offered him a permanent position as director of the kitchens of the Ferrières estate, which he had just bought, Carême replied: "My prayer is not to end my days in a château, but in humble lodgings in Paris. And to publish a comprehensive survey of the state of my profession at the present time."

He still had a helpful word for the poor: "It is an error for those of lesser station to try to pattern their tables after the rich." Instead he urged them to serve simple meals of fewer courses "and not try to cover the bourgeois table with an imitation of *les grands.* "

It saddened him that Napoleon was reduced to eating mainly bananas on St. Helena, and he sent a note to the chef there to soak them in rum and then fry them in batter to make a *beignet*. On the other hand, his recipe for *grosses meringues à la Parisienne* ran to seven pages.

Carême agreed with La Reynière that "leftover" was an unmentionable word, and that any host who salvaged unfinished food to use again was no Amphitryon. That name, originally from Greek mythology, refers in this case to the generous host. "For a rich man," wrote Grimod, "the best role in the world is that of host." But "the world visits his dinners and not him," Molière observed.

Some say that the controversy over service *à la française* and service *à la russe* derived from Carême's having been employed at the court of Czar Alexander, sent, it is rumored, by Talleyrand to gather military secrets. Actually, however, Carême espoused the French way because it allowed him the chance to display his *pièces montées* to the best advantage, and his roasts, galantines, aspics, and chartreuses to be admired intact rather than carved. Otherwise where was the incentive to create them?

"A well-displayed meal is enhanced one hundred percent in my eyes," he said. As for the chartreuse, a molded, decorated dish of partridges and fresh vegetables, Carême called it "undoubtedly the queen of entrées one can serve."

Originated during the reign of Louis XIV, service *à la française* designated that all dishes offered to the guests be set out on an immense table in an impressive and overwhelming still-life array. While the guests were being impressed and overwhelmed, hot food was growing cool and chilled food was melting. But this was far from the only disadvantage.

One sat at this table wherever the host and the salt cellar ordained. It made no difference whether one cared for what happened to be set before one; one dined on that, or at very best what was within polite grasp.

It mattered not whether one's favorite *saumon à la Génoise* or *turban de filets mignons* was ornately featured down the table; if it could not easily be reached, it could only be stared at with longing. Guests were allowed no passing of platters back and forth, and there were no waiters. Once the footmen had set the food in place, their duties were over until they removed the plates.

A lady guest might neither reach nor beseech. Dazzled by countless temptations, she had to wait until the gentlemen at her side inquired what (close by) she would like. If she was disregarded, it has been reported, she might end up with nothing for dinner but the dish of peas before her. "Contentment," mourned an observer, "was out of the question."

Pure chance, therefore, regulated whether one enjoyed, or did not enjoy, escalloped hazel-grouse in aspic, black-truffled capon, saddle of young hare, partridges on a bed of foie gras, or venison cutlets *à la gelée d'oranges*. But the disappointed gourmet could still console himself that an evening of *"fortune du pot"* in which he had supped upon grilled turbot with oyster sauce, a soufflé of *pigeons innocents,* and *tartelettes glacées aux pistaches Carême* could not be considered a total loss.

Still, it was inevitable that this ostentatious and unsatisfactory manner of offering food should resolve itself into a method by which seated guests were served in rotation by footmen passing platters to one and all alike. The meat was cut up, and there was enough for most. Hot food remained reasonably hot, and although there was not the variety of the spreads *à la française,* at least each guest had a chance to sample them all. The new method was called service *à la russe.*

As if anticipating this, at the Royal Pavillion John Nash had designed a "Decker's Room" between the Great Kitchen and the Banqueting Hall, where the *chefs de cuisine* could set down the platters to be picked up by the footmen. Dishes containing boiling water helped to keep the entrées warm. The dining table itself was decorated mainly with candelabra, cutlery, porcelain, and crystal, and inevitably a few set-pieces.

The chief proponent of service *à la russe* was the author of *La Cuisine Classique,* Felix Urbain-Dubois, chef of the King of Prussia and the court of Germany. Carême, who had observed this fashion under the Czar and rejected it because he preferred to mass the dining table with his sculpted creations, would have agreed that the new arrangement was more pleasing to the guests, who ultimately preferred eating to viewing.

Footmen, or waiters, as they began to be called, came into their own with service *à la russe.* Hitherto relegated to the background, they now moved freely back and forth between the sideboards and the guests, many times even recommending a particular delicacy, or daring to serve an especially succulent portion to some favored patron. The era of the importance of the waiter had begun.

Meanwhile, the Czar from whose court the trend emerged had died, reportedly of mushroom poisoning, like Pope Clement. These were not fungi prepared by his famous chef, but, old superstition says, "the ones found growing near serpent holes or rusty nails." Czar Alexander's version was that he was "crushed beneath the terrible burden of a crown."

That same year, 1825, saw a remarkable volume appear in France. *La Physiologie du Goût (The Physiology of Taste)* was written not by a chef at all but by a provincial lawyer and mayor of the small town of Belley, in Burgundy, where he was born in 1755 on April Fool's Day.

Anything but a fool, Jean Anthelme Brillat-Savarin, an ardent gastronome, also published works on law and political economics, and entertained his friends Talleyrand, Balzac, Sainte-Beuve, Victor Hugo, and other *bon vivants* with his violin and with his table. For several decades he had been working on a book filled with pungent accounts of memorable meals he had enjoyed, and suggestions about how to prepare them. His recipe for fondue, given him in Switzerland, begins: "Take as many eggs as you wish, according to the number of guests, and weigh them," and ends: "Bring out the best wine, and let it go round freely, and wonders will be done."

Other culinary observations include: "If a figpecker [a small golden warbler frequenting fig orchards] could grow as big as a pheasant, it would be worth the price of an acre of land . . . When sportsmen in the Dauphiné hunt in September, they too are armed with salt and with pepper. If one of them happens to bag a plump, perfect figpecker he plucks it, seasons it, carries it for a time in the crown of his hat, and eats it. Such gourmands insist that this is much more delicious than the bird when roasted."

He devised rather cruel jests for testing "gastric sensitivity." One was to inform his guests that a promised hamper of game had not arrived *(à la Vatel)* and then judge their gourmet qualities on the basis of their apparent disappointment.

Actually Carême took a dim view of Brillat-Savarin's own qualifications as a gourmet, claiming he recommended "strong and vulgar things," ate too much, spoke too little, and after dinner "I have seen him fall asleep." Furthermore, he "resembled a parson."

Perhaps at the source of Carême's disapproval was a meal presented by this Mayor of Belley that began with a bouillon of veal and then featured the veal itself. Or perhaps it was simply that uncooked figpecker.

In any case, Jean Anthelme Brillat-Savarin's most enduring contribution seems to have been the sprinkling of aphorisms with which his treatise is seasoned. Among the most famous of these are: "The discovery of a new dish does more for human happiness than the discovery of a new star." "Tell me what you eat, and I shall tell you what you are." And "Animals feed; men eat; gourmets alone know how to dine."

Of him, his friend Balzac wrote that he could outride the storms of revolution and intrigue and never let them trouble his digestion. And upon Brillat-Savarin's death in 1826, only a year after the publication of *La Physiologie du Goût,* an admirer remarked that he "left the world like a satisfied diner leaving the banquet room."

Embraced by society at about this time was one of the most delightful of all repasts, the picnic. The word itself is supposed to have come from the old French *pique* (to "pick" or "peck") and *nique* ("a trifle"). The *Larousse Gastronomique* defines it as "a meal taken in the open, or a meal to which each participant contributes a dish." The expression is said to have come into being around the end of the seventeenth century, perhaps with peasants eating their midday meal in the fields, perhaps with a king's hunting party refreshing itself in a wooded glade.

*Fêtes champêtres,* or *déjeuners sur l'herbe* or *sous l'arbre* were studiedly simple at the time of the Louis', the nobility dressing and posing as shepherds and milk-maids. It was not until Carême came to Brighton that the concept of *"le pique-nique"* reached the British. The court was entranced. Along the Promenade and beside the sea, aristocrats who had never heard of the "ploughman's lunch" of bread, cheese, and beer dis-covered the delights of eating with their fingers and in the open air sliced truffled pheasant and French bread coated with foie gras.

Even the Prince Regent was charmed, and formed his exclusive "Picnic Club," for which Carême may have prepared any or all of these essentials laid down by Grimod de la Reynière in 1806 for a repast alfresco "lasting about four hours" to be enjoyed by "six ladies and six gentlemen":

> A fricassee of some nice fat chicken, put in a loaf of bread.

2 large galantines, one of beef tongue, the other of a nice hare.

A very nice roast of young turkey, cold.

A good Mayence or Bayonne ham, well cooked and trimmed.

A nice pâté of boned pullets, accompanied by either quail or larks according to season.

A covered pastry of partridge, well garnished.

A nice almond cream tart.

A very fine *biscuit de Savoie.*

A well-cleaned salad with oil and vinegar in bottles and a napkin to toss it when it has been seasoned.

Coffee, sugar, mustard.

Fruits in season, some plates of *petits fours,* cookies, macaroons, comfits, and, for the men, Gruyère or Roquefort.

6 bottles of ordinary wine, 2 bottles of Jurançon, 2 of Champagne, 1 bottle of Malaga, 1 of Frontignan, and 2 of liqueur.

It obviously lived up to the Oxford Dictionary's definition of a "fashionable social entertainment," a "pleasure party in which all take part of a repast out of doors."

That indefatigable commentator on the gastronomic scene, Brillat-Savarin, had his say on the subject: ". . . the world is our dining room and the sun itself is our light. And what is more, appetite, that heaven-sent emanation, gives to this feast a liveliness unknown to tight-shut rooms . . ."

And what does *he* recommend? ". . . the treasures of Périgord, the marvels of Strasbourg, the dainties of Archard . . . and potent champagne."

Also the company of ladies. "I have watched them spread out upon the grass the plates of turkey in transparent jelly, the homemade pâté, the salad waiting to be tossed in its bowl . . . this gypsy feasting, and I am thoroughly convinced that there is no less charm about it for its lack of luxury."

Antonin Carême, however, continued to be surrounded by elegance. He worked at the Court of Vienna, at the British Embassy in Paris, and at the Congress of Aix-la-Chapelle. The Baron Rothschild hired him "at a salary beyond what any soverign in Europe might be able to pay," and Carême praised the "delicate luxury" of the Baroness's table at the Château de Boulogne.

And yet, in spite of an undisputed pomposity reflected in his edible sculptures, his grandiloquent prose style, and his self-assurance, he readily acknowledged his indebtedness to his teachers. "It was under M. Richaut, the famous sauce cook of the House of Condé, that I learned the preparation of sauces; during the splendid festivities held at the Hôtel de Ville in Paris, under the orders of M. Lasne, that I learned the best part of cold buffet cookery, at the Elysée Napoleon under the auspices of Messrs. Robert and Laguipière that I learned the elegance of modern cookery and the working of a large establishment."

Carême died in 1833 before his fiftieth birthday,

burned out, a colleague said, "by the flame of his genius and the fuel of his ovens." For years he had denounced coal as the greatest enemy of the chef. "This charcoal is killing us," he wrote, "but what does it matter? *Moins de jours et plus de gloire* (the fewer the days, the greater the glory)."

"This den . . . this terrifying kitchen, is filled with noise day and night. In its little cage, hooked to the master beam, sleeps a tiny bird, regardless of the din and the stifling heat."

*Oeufs Carême* appear on menus from time to time. There are numerous variations. Generally they are halves of hard-cooked eggs filled with a mixture of the yolks and some kind of fish (usually cod or salmon), coated with white sauce and baked or browned. Escoffier mentions *oeufs durs Carême* (a timbale crust containing sliced hard-cooked eggs, artichoke bottoms, and truffles in a *sauce Nantua*), and also *oeufs froids Carême* (cold poached eggs in pastry shells covered with salmon in mayonnaise, and caviar and black truffles. The *Larousse Gastronomique* lists three different versions.

Every year a group that calls itself "The Disciples of Antonin Carême" meets for lunch. A recent menu might have seemed strange to the honoree, not because of the quality, but for the quantity of its courses. The Disciples dined simply upon: *foie gras parfait,* sole soufflé *Abel Luquet,* saddle of lamb *Antonin Carême,* Cointreau sherbet, cold sliced Nantes duck with orange, cheeses, and *omelette Duc de Praslin.*

The wines are not listed, so we can only imagine what was in the glasses when they were raised in grateful praise of the supreme chef of the years before Escoffier.

# 3

★ ★ ★ ★

## ESCOFFIER:
## THE BEGINNINGS

*"A master cook! why, he is the man of men."*
*Ben Jonson*

As a special treat on his son's thirteenth birthday, the blacksmith of Villeneuve-Loubet in the Alpes Maritimes region of France took the boy to dinner in a restaurant. Until then the only meals Georges Auguste Escoffier had enjoyed outside of his mother's fragrant kitchen were picnic lunches along the road to Antibes, where his father, who also raised tobacco, sold his crop. There in the herb-scented meadows of Provence they would dine upon coarse homemade pâté, sardines, local goat cheese, crusty bread with olive oil and garlic, and fruit. Sometimes the boy was allowed a glass of *vin du pays,* while the donkey pulling the cart of tobacco leaves grazed on wild thyme and fennel.

But the twenty-eighth of October 1859 found Auguste seated at a table in Le Restaurant Français, a popular establishment in Nice. The restaurant belonged to his father's brother. And at the boy's request, his uncle had placed him near the kitchen, where, when the door swung open, he could see the perspiring chefs with their battery of pots and pans. He could also see piles of glistening eggplants, sweet peppers, and mushrooms; bowls of ripe olives in their oil; baskets of oranges, greengages, and figs; strings of garlic and ropes of onions; branches of herbs; platters of silvery fish outlined in parsley and rimmed with lemons; anchovies in mustard; spiny sea urchins, langoustes; huge wheels of cheese; and open pots redolent with *aïoli*.

His uncle observed the boy's face. Nice was becoming more and more fashionable; a large crowd was expected for the winter; honest and hard-working waiters were difficult to find. He asked his nephew if he would like to stay on as a waiter.

Auguste replied that he would rather work in the kitchen.

Father and uncle smiled, and then the father pointed out that his son was too slight of stature to carry the heavy dining room trays. Quickly Auguste Escoffier thanked his uncle and told him he would be proud to serve as a waiter in his restaurant.

Nice, upon whose harbor Caterina de' Medici had gazed on the way to her wedding three hundred years before, lies near the border of Italy, and the Italian influence has always pervaded its cuisine. The highly suspect tomato *(pomo d'oro,* "golden apple," of the Italians, and "love apple" of the British, from the French *pomme de Moor,* "Moorish apple," which the British interpreted as *pomme d'amour)* had crossed the border. So had some forms of pasta. Genoa's *pesto* undoubtedly led to Nice's *soupe au pistou,* a thick basil-and-garlic-flavored vegetable soup with noodles, similar to minestrone, another derivative from Italy.

The term *"niçoise"* indicates the presence of olive oil, garlic, and tomatoes, whose scents permeate the air of this part of France. Often black olives, anchovies, a whiff of tarragon, a grind of pepper, a crumble of saffron, or a strip of pimiento will indicate a Mediterranean cuisine more highly seasoned and individual than that of much of the rest of France.

It was no wonder that the thirteen-year-old waiter was entranced.

It was also no wonder that with such provocative odors emanating from the kitchen of Le Restaurant Français the boy spent more and more of his free time there, time in which he was allowed to skim a soup, or stir a stew, or baste a roast. Long accustomed to the blaze of his father's forge, he did not object to the heat of the stoves, and the chefs began giving him menial jobs.

After five years, to his uncle's astonishment, the boy

was organizing the kitchen staff, ordering provisions and going to market, and passing final judgment on special entrées to be presented to diners. More than once he was observed removing an unsuitable garnish from a plate and substituting one of his own devising, because most of all he longed to be a cook, to prepare a famous dish or invent a new one. It was not long before news of this reached the nearby Hôtel Bellevue.

Young Escoffier's uncle was loath to part with him; he was fond of the boy and recognized his diligence, imagination, and ambition. But he had no *sous-chef's* job open for him, and the hotel had. The older Escoffier let Auguste go with his blessing.

At the Bellevue, Auguste learned the principles of sauce making, roasting, and patisserie. There were moments when he believed he knew all there was to know about being a chef. At other times he despaired of ever being anything but an apprentice, and he wondered if he should not perhaps return to Villeneuve to help his father, or even go to Arles to paint. Then one afternoon something happened to change all that.

He was crossing the garden of the hotel when he noticed one of the guests, a frail-looking girl about his age, stretched out on a long chair in the shade of a eucalyptus. He had seen her there before, but this time she beckoned to him and asked if he was the cook.

"I am one of the cooks," Auguste told her.

"There is something I want so much," she went on. "I have not seen it on the menu, yet I am sure it must be here." Politely he asked her what it was that she wished.

"You will laugh," she said. "It is so simple. Too simple to place on the menu, yet it would taste so good to me. A little cold white meat of chicken, perfectly plain, with fruit beside. That is all. You are laughing."

Auguste, who was not laughing, returned to the kitchen, prepared a chicken breast *chaud-froid,* and set a chilled poached pear beside it. As he was recrossing the lawn with the tray, something caught his eye, and on an impulse he bent down, picked a violet, and laid it across the pear.

A few days later the girl's father called him to his room. "I understand that you have met my daughter," he said.

Auguste mumbled that he had brought her some cold chicken at her request. For some reason, the thought of the violet rested uncomfortably in his mind.

The man went on to explain that his daughter, Hélène, had been desperately ill in Paris, and that he had brought her south to recuperate in the mild climate of the Riviera. Because of the rich food at the hotel, she had made no progress at first. Now, thanks to Escoffier, she was beginning to eat again. Her father would like to repay the young cook.

The idea of being paid by the guests to provide

satisfactory meals was appalling to Auguste. He was even more appalled when this stranger suggested that because of his concern for people's health he might consider becoming a physician. Auguste blurted out that what he wanted to become was a great chef.

The stranger introduced himself as M. Bardoux, proprietor of the Restaurant du Petit Moulin Rouge in the rue d'Antin. He was, therefore, in a position to reward the young man after all. By chance there happened to be a situation open for a *rôtisseur*.

That was in 1865. To Georges Auguste Escoffier, dreaming of becoming a great chef, Paris was the ultimate goal. Once there, though, he found little time for dreaming.

The kitchen of the Petit Moulin Rouge was presided over by the autocratic Ulysse Rohan, who believed in and insisted on the strictest discipline for the excellence he expected. The relaxed days of sunny Provence were over, and the nineteen-year-old apprentice roast cook worked tirelessly.

Always small, he wore built-up heels to lift him above the coke-burning ovens, and sometimes he stood on a block of wood. This was a source of considerable scorn and amusement among his colleagues; rivalry ran high and so did tempers. But with his quiet good manners and intelligence, and his desire to please, Auguste easily made friends. Jean Giroix, a fellow chef, was one of them.

Antonin Carême once recognized sauces as the hall-mark of the classic French cuisine. By 1870, Escoffier had advanced to sauce chef.

That same year France was at war with Germany, and Escoffier was sent to Metz in the Lorraine as *chef de cuisine* at the Rhine Army Headquarters. All of his ingenuity was instantly challenged. There was simply not enough food, a fact which the demanding officers were unwilling to accept, even though the Jardin des Plantes, Paris's zoo, was selling its animals—kangaroo, bear, and antelope—to the restaurants because it could no longer feed them; and the Jardin d'Acclimatation had sent the trunks of its pet elephants, Castor and Pollux, to the fashionable Café Voisin to appear as *trompe, sauce chasseur* to the unabashed dismay of diners who had once offered them peanuts.

Dining on hansom-cab horsemeat became inevitable in the siege, although Edmond de Goncourt, critic and historian of the period, claimed that it gave him night-mares, and "I fell back on a couple of larks." On the battlefield Escoffier made it palatable by scalding it first, then cooling it before braising. Courageously he assessed it as "delicious when one is in the right cir-cumstances to appreciate it."

Potatoes were scarce; he substituted truffles. Mira-belle jam took the place of sugar. "Fortunately my hens were laying a little. I used the eggs in every conceivable way, boiled, served on a bed of chicory, or as often as not with minced horse-meat . . ."

Grilled goat and pig pâté appeared in the Mess from time to time. Once, in August, near Gravelotte, the young chef caught a rabbit and simmered it in white wine and cognac. "The rabbit which figures in my menu would surely deserve a place in the annals of that campaign, under the name of *le lapin de Gravelotte,* not only by virtue of being the only remaining rabbit in that part of the country, but also for the manner in which it was served." The officers, "who had had to learn to make do with little, found the result delicious."

Always seeking to please his men, Escoffier must have found the constant lack of suitable ingredients frustrating beyond words. And the situation grew steadily worse. "On the day Metz surrendered," he wrote, "there remained one chicken, a jar of meat extract, a tin of tunny fish, and the goat, which I sold."

At the end of the Franco-Prussian War in 1871, Escoffier returned to the Petit Moulin Rouge, where he became head chef. It remained a stylish and popular place. The young Prince of Wales, who much later was to become King Edward VII, dined there now and then. When Escoffier prepared a special dish for him, it is unlikely that he ever imagined that in thirty years he would be supervising his Coronation Banquet.

It would appear that Auguste had achieved his highest goal. But there was always something more; he now dreamed of a restaurant of his own. He discussed it with M. Bardoux and with his uncle in Nice whose

Restaurant Français was still enjoying great success.

His uncle was enthusiastic about the future of the Riviera. The development of the railroads with their luxurious sleeping cars and appointments, and even fairly good food, was bringing a wealthy and expectant clientele to the Mediterranean seeking the sun, the beaches, the sea air. Cannes was becoming a popular resort of both the French and English aristocracy. So in 1879 Georges Auguste Escoffier opened his own establishment there, Le Faisan Doré.

Because he believed that "a cook's first duty is to conform to the desires of Amphytrions and customers," and that his second is to educate them and raise their standards and levels of taste, and also because he was already recognized as a superb chef, Escoffier's Golden Pheasant was instantly acclaimed. Not only did "Amphytrions and customers" from Cannes flock to it, but the Prince of Wales came from Menton, and Charles III, Prince of Monaco, from Monte Carlo. One day another visitor arrived from Monte Carlo.

He was the manager of the Grand Hôtel there. Escoffier had been too preoccupied with his own restaurant to dine at the Grand, but he knew of its reputation for fine cuisine; its head chef was none other than Jean Giroix, his colleague from the Petit Moulin Rouge, who had once defined a gourmet as "a man who knows what he wants and wants only the best." Escoffier congratulated the manager on his choice.

But Giroix, it appeared, was leaving. The rival

Hôtel de Paris had offered him what the manager of
the Grand, in no mood for bargaining, called an "absurd sum." In any case, he already had a replacement
in mind, a man recommended by none other than His
Royal Highness the Prince of Wales, as well as by
Giroix himself. He had come to Le Faisan Doré in
person to invite Escoffier to join him.

Escoffier was dismayed. He had just achieved his
life's dream, and although his restaurant could hardly
be called sumptuous, it was exactly what he desired
and made him supremely content. The general manager of the Grand Hôtel, which was also not sumptuous nor even particularly well built, laid down his
calling card and begged the chef to reconsider. Years
later, his widow, Mme César Ritz, was to write that the
collaboration of these two men was the most fortunate
event in their lives.

César Ritz was born in 1850, four years after Escoffier, in the remote Swiss alpine village of Nierder-
wald, "a huddle of weatherbeaten wooden cottages
clinging to the mountainside above the upper reaches
of the icy, rushing Rhone . . . in a forest of evergreens,
and below, flowering meadows. On a clear day," Marie Louise Ritz continues in her biography of her husband, "one can see the Jungfrau."

His father owned a small farm with a few goats and
cows—"there was always the sound of the wind in the

treetops, and cow-bells . . ." César was his thirteenth child, and superstitious about that all his life.

As in the case of Carême, money was needed and children were not. M. Ritz offered three hundred francs to a friend with an establishment in the nearby town of Brig if he would hire his son. So at fifteen César Ritz became an apprentice wine waiter at the Hôtel des Trois Couronnes et Poste. He was soon dismissed for lacking "a special flair." He would never make anything of himself in the hotel business, M. Escher, the proprietor, informed the boy's father.

When the Great Exhibition opened in Paris in 1867, Ritz went there looking for work, and found a job carrying bags and trays at the Hôtel de la Fidélité in the Boulevard du Prince Eugène . . . "Hotel, Boulevard, and Prince all long since forgotten," says Mme Ritz.

Several restaurants later (he broke dishes because he hurried), he had developed sufficient "flair" to be hired at the elegant Café Voisin. "One quick head is worth a dozen pairs of quick feet, my boy," counseled M. Bellenger, the proprietor.

As a waiter there, he served George Sand, Sarah Bernhardt, and Alexandre Dumas, among other famous customers. During the Siege of Paris he might even have carried the platters of elephant's trunk in hunter's sauce, not to mention *chat accompagné de rats.*

Later, as maître d'hôtel of the Splendide on the

Place de l'Opéra, he catered to the entourage of the Prince of Wales, who, like an earlier Prince of Wales, was fond of good food and fair ladies. "You know better than I do what I like," Albert Edward told César. And Ritz began to realize that he had a talent for pleasing the royal and the wealthy. His insistence on perfection at any cost attracted them. They came where he was, moving with the seasons like migrating birds, and he was quick to establish himself at their gathering places.

At the International Exhibition in Vienna he served the Emperor Franz Joseph at the Imperial Pavilion. When he was twenty-three years old, summertime found him at the Grand Hôtel National in Lucerne; the winter at the Grand in Monte Carlo.

With Escoffier, however reluctantly, at the Grand, it soon surpassed its rival, the newly decorated and newly chefed Hôtel de Paris. Queen Victoria drove from Menton for lunch in a private dining room; her son was a constant guest. Others included King Frederick VIII of Denmark, the Emperor Franz Joseph and the Empress Elizabeth, the Empress Eugènie, Dom Pedro of Brazil, and the grand dukes and duchesses of Russia.

Why did they come? Years later Mme Ritz was to write: "The supremacy of the hotel relied on its magnificent cuisine and impeccable management. The building itself was not architecturally fine, nor was its decoration outstanding . . . Indeed, during a slight tremor, two partitions crumbled to the ground."

The Baroness Rothschild, whose apartment was in ruins, remained a faithful client. So did Swedish princes, South African and American millionaires, and Oriental potentates.

Ritz's own explanation was that "M. Escoffier is undoubtedly the finest chef in the world."

Besides beautiful ladies and fine dining, the Prince of Wales had another keen interest: race horses. As a gesture of congratulation for one of his thoroughbreds' running of the Derby, Escoffier created and served to him one evening in 1881 a dish that was to assure the Prince's eternal favor and the Grand Hôtel's international fame. A *poularde Derby* was a roast chicken stuffed with rice, chopped truffles, and foie gras; and garnished with sautéed slices of foie gras on croutons and whole truffles simmered in meat jelly and Madeira.

The Prince, who had requested "something light, but interesting," and was always fond of a well-roasted bird, declared it "a truly royal dish."

*Poularde Grand Hôtel* was invented to please those more eager to return to the gaming tables at the casino than to wait for a truffle-stuffed pullet. The chicken was cut up, cooked quickly, and served in a *cocotte* with sliced truffles on top.

Escoffier's *poularde à la Monte Carlo* was a poached

pullet coated with *sauce suprême,* and surrounded by pink quenelles of chicken and "very black" truffles.

Trains arrived regularly now at the Côte d'Azur: the Orient Express; *Le Train Bleu,* an all-sleeper train from Paris to the Riviera; the Calais-Rome Express; and the South and North Expresses. By 1884 restaurant cars were serving excellent and expensive meals, putting the passengers in the mood for more. They had come to the right place.

One of those who came was Felix Urbain-Dubois, the chef at the German court who had advocated service *à la russe* to take the place of the service *à la française* employed by Carême. Escoffier was eager to meet him, and Urbain-Dubois, who had heard of the young man's skill, urged him to write down some of his recipes. Unlike Carême, Auguste had no desire to write. Painting was still what he longed to have time to do; he had also enjoyed shaping flowers of wax. In the huge gloomy kitchen of the Grand, the two chefs discussed their profession.

Urbain-Dubois, who had published *La Cuisine Classique* and *Cuisine Artistique,* suggested that Escoffier at least list the principal ingredients of his dishes so the headwaiters could advise the diners. Escoffier thought of the helter-skelter clutter of notes jammed into the pigeonholes of his desk. To organize them seemed totally unlikely, if not altogether impossible.

One morning Escoffier's old benefactor, M. Bardoux, called to say that he was bringing his daughter, Hélène, to dine. Escoffier would recall the simplicity of her tastes, said Bardoux, and perhaps for the sweet course he would serve something, shall we say, romantic?

Escoffier himself brought the dessert to their table. He had lined a charlotte mold with meringue shells and filled the center with whipped cream tinted with tangerine syrup. When frozen and turned out, he had poured Chantilly cream on it. Then, on an impulse, he had scattered crystallized violets over the top.

Hélène was enchanted. "So, monsieur, what is it called, this alluring dish of yours?"

The chef requested permission to name it *mousse Hélène.*

"But people would ask, who is she, this Hélène? I am not famous. I suggest that you call it *mousse Monte Carlo* for the place that made *you* famous."

There were other desserts to be composed by Escoffier in the Grand's kitchen: *brise d'avril* (April breeze), made of strawberries, kirsch, and *crème Chantilly,* also with pralined violets; *bombe Monte Carlo,* a mold lined with vanilla ice cream, filled with strawberry mousse, and served with whole strawberries in Curaçao; and *beignets en fleurs d'acacia,* fresh acacia blossoms drenched in Kirsch, fried in batter, and sprinkled with sugar. He recommended the same process for elder flowers and day lilies.

There was no doubt that Escoffier enjoyed creating dishes for women, probably because so few would dine in public, and he and César Ritz were anxious to lure them to their hotel restaurants. For Sarah Bernhardt, who loved strawberries, he invented two special desserts. *Soufflé Sarah Bernhardt* was a vanilla-flavored cream custard baked with macaroons soaked in Curaçao, then covered with strawberry purée and *crème Chantilly* and served with whole strawberries in Curaçao. "Custard permits of all the flavoring essences," he said, "but the one which suits it best is vanilla."

*Fraises Sarah Bernhardt* were large strawberries, dipped in orange-flavored liqueur, surrounding a pineapple mousse topped with a Curaçao mousse and served with macaroons! It is truly a marvel that the Divine Sarah maintained her boyish figure.

For the Empress Elizabeth he made a vanilla cream soufflé, arranged in alternate layers with pralined violets and macaroons soaked in kirsch, the whole enmeshed in a net of spun sugar. And for the Empress Eugènie (for whom he also prepared a famous "rice pudding," *Riz à l'Imperatrice*) there were Montreuil peaches with wild strawberries, sprinkled with kirsch and maraschino, and covered with a *sabayon* made with champagne. *Sabayon* is the French version of the *zabaglione* brought from Florence by Catherine de Médicis.

*Pêches Alexandra,* dedicated to the beautiful wife of

the Prince of Wales, were poached in vanilla syrup, placed on vanilla ice cream, covered with maraschino-flavored strawberry purée, and strewn with crystallized rose petals.

In the winter of 1888, César Ritz married Marie Louise Rosnoblet, his "Mimi," in Cannes. He was thirty-seven; she was twenty. They had met five years before, while her mother was manager of the Hôtel de Monte Carlo.

The Ritzes moved into an apartment in Baden-Baden above the Restaurant de la Conversation, which César had just bought. Opening night saw the restaurant transformed into a bower of tropical plants, with the innovation of tiny electric lights shining from the leaves and branches.

Escoffier, whom they could not yet "afford," stayed on at the Grand, moving in summertime to the Grand Hôtel National in Lucerne. Both hotels continued to attract the royal, the aristocratic, and the wealthy of many lands.

"The National became a great hotel only when Escoffier took over the management of the kitchens," Ritz would say. To which, with his modest manner and gentle, discerning expression, Escoffier would answer: "Good cooking is the foundation of true happiness."

This particular happiness was destined to come to a momentary and unexpected end. It came in the form of a forty-four-year-old London-born Irishman named Richard D'Oyly Carte.

Like the Prince of Wales, D'Oyly Carte regularly came to Baden-Baden to "take the waters." At a party at the Restaurant de la Conversation, he met César Ritz, who had once again succeeded in turning the dining room into a "woodland scene." Having persuaded the horticultural gardens to lend him a giant tree fern, he had had a huge round table built around it, carpeted the floor with turf, and installed a fountain and a goldfish pond.

D'Oyly Carte was impressed both by Ritz's imagination and by the theatrical quality of the setting. He said that he would like to see "this kind of thing" in London. For in 1881 D'Oyly Carte had opened the Savoy Theatre in the Strand, the only one in England to boast electric lighting, produced by an engine "chugging away in a nearby shed." The first production there was an operetta called *Patience,* written by his partners, W. S. Gilbert and Arthur Sullivan. Tea and cakes were offered to those waiting in line for tickets.

Of the Savoy, D'Oyly Carte wrote after opening night: "The new theatre is a colossal success, the loveliest theatre *in the world* all the critics say and everyone. Acoustics marvellous. In the top gallery every whisper is heard. Electric light in the auditorium only—stage will be lighted next week with it. At the end of the show the top gallery as *cool* as a sitting room with two wax candles."

Actually it was "the end of the show" that was the chief concern of Richard D'Oyly Carte now that his dream theater was a reality. Where would his audience dine afterward; how would they spend the rest of the evening? In his opinion there was no restaurant that matched the elegance and beauty of his theater in the Strand. And furthermore, he figured, if there was a suitable hotel nearby, customers from the Counties might be persuaded to come to London for the operettas and spend the night.

A review a year later only strengthened his resolve. "The Savoy Theatre, lighted like no other theatre in Europe, and looking exceptionally brilliant on this occasion, was crammed to its utmost capacity." Included in the throng were the Prince of Wales and Prime Minister Gladstone.

D'Oyly Carte began to plan his Savoy Hotel. The land in the old "Savoie Mannor," behind the theater, was a sloping field overgrown with weeds and littered with bottles; it looked out upon coal wharves and barges, all the flotsam and jetsam of the Thames Embankment. Standing in the field, D'Oyly Carte stared across the litter to where the majestic river moved and knew that he had the location he wanted for his establishment.

Construction began in 1884. Concrete was poured for the first time in a British hotel. As they always do, observers gathered to watch and offer their opinions. The artist Whistler sketched the scaffolding and remarked that the building would never look so well again.

On the sixth of August 1889 the hotel opened. Several days before, D'Oyly Carte ran an advertisement in *The Times* describing the fireproof steel frame, the power plant for electricity, the artesian well, the sixty-seven bathrooms. London's leading hotel, until then, had four. "The perfection of luxury and comfort," raved the advertisement. "Artistic furniture throughout. The Hotel enjoys the finest river and garden view in London, it has wide balconies running all along the front, commanding a panorama of the Thames, with its many features of interest from Battersea to London Bridge, embracing St. Paul's Cathedral, the Monument, the Tower of London, the Surrey Hills, the Crystal Palace, the Houses of Parliament, Westminster Abbey, and the various bridges." *The Illustrated London News* agreed that "nothing is wanted to please the educated eye or gratify the taste."

The opening of the Savoy was planned to coincide with the marriage of Louise, oldest daughter of the Prince of Wales, and the Duke of Fife. To the hotel came royalty from many countries; among those registered were the Shah of Persia, the Emperor of Germany, and the King of Greece. The cuisine was predominantly Continental, but, presumably to please American guests, clams, terrapin, corn, and pumpkin pie also appeared on the menu.

Yet the advertised "perfection of luxury and comfort" left a great deal to be desired, particularly in the kitchen. The Prince of Wales himself complained that the cooking was as dull as Windsor Castle's. D'Oyly Carte knew that there was only one person who could change this.

He had dined at the Grand with Sarah Bernhardt, the de Reszkes, Patti, and Coquelin, so he was not unfamiliar with the talents of César Ritz when he came across him in Baden-Baden. Actually, his good friend Lily Langtry had urged him to approach Ritz, prophesying that he would attract ladies to his hotel. By 1888 D'Oyly Carte was in a position to ask Ritz to manage the new Savoy, scheduled to open the next winter. "There's not a hotel in London where you can get a decent meal . . . much less dine like a god as one does here," he added persuasively.

Ritz wasted no time in declining the offer. To him, the prospect of England was less than godly. Aside from the fogs that had depressed Carême, there were unfavorable trade-union regulations, restricted licensing and dining hours, and further "puritanical" conventions. He also understood that the British distrusted foreigners and foreign food, and that gentlemen of quality dined chiefly in their clubs.

In his long theatrical experience, D'Oyly Carte was accustomed to coping with what he deemed temperament and unreasonableness. Persistence and praise were his weapons. "You are the finest hotel manager in the world; I shall have the finest hotel. The two belong together."

Marie Louise called him "the wily old Irishman." "He thinks your name alone can do it," she said.

"It will attract the crowds he wants," Ritz told her, "but it won't keep them."

Then M. and Mme Ritz received an invitation to come to the Savoy for a week as D'Oyly Carte's guests to help celebrate the hotel's inauguration. There would be balls and banquets, and a new operetta, *The Gondoliers,* opening at the theater. All expenses would be paid, and naturally there would be no commitment to remain beyond the seven days.

Because of her expected baby, Marie Louise could not accept.

"The food will be horrible and the weather worse," her husband consoled her.

"But to see the new hotel, all electric, the greatest in Europe, in the world . . ."

"*His* opinion only."

"The ideas, the novelties, the temptations you can bring back to introduce in our hotels here." She was as persuasive as the Irishman.

César, ever eager to please her, admitted, "The omens are good for the Savoy. But I go only as a brief holiday."

Escoffier also encouraged Ritz. For too many years

he had been distressed by the gloom and heat and noise of his kitchens. Even though he might never use it, he was anxious to hear at first hand what differences electricity would bring.

Ritz returned in a state of excitement and awe. Never had he seen so many diamonds on so many beautiful women. "Wealth! Wealth! on every side . . . from Persia, India, Africa, America . . . M. D'Oyly Carte was correct . . ."

What about the *hotel?* Marie Louise wanted to know.

The excitement and awe faded. "It will not succeed," he said. "Not under its present management."

He described the comfort and luxury of his suite with its "vast marble bathroom," the six elevators paneled in Chinese-red lacquer, the brilliant lighting throughout, the excellent equipment of the kitchens. "But the cuisine was uninteresting," he told Escoffier. "The thing will fail."

It almost did. Ritz was offered the managership at his own price.

"Only if I may bring Escoffier," he said.

"Never," replied Escoffier.

It has been eloquently stated that with the herbs, native fruits, and spices "growing in profusion and without cultivation over her rocks . . . the Provençal digestions are tranquilised and her populations content to stay at home."

A few weeks later Escoffier received a letter from London. "I need you, *mon vieux.*"

With a heavy heart, Georges Auguste Escoffier packed up his few personal belongings and his omelet pan, and made the journey.

# 4

★ ★ ★ ★

## THE SAVOY YEARS

*"Oh, the roast beef of England,*
*And old England's roast beef!"*
Henry Fielding

Since the brief reign of Antonin Carême over the royal kitchens of the Prince Regent, the influence of French cuisine had not spread far in Britain. Englishmen still distrusted foreign food, particularly French, believing that it consisted largely of frivolous, elaborately named *quelque chose,* "something" of this and that, instead of a decent meal. Their anglicization, "kickshaw," still means, often contemptuously, "a fancy dish in cookery . . . but insubstantial." Actually it goes back to Shakespeare's day. He wrote of "A joynt of Mutton, and any pretty little tinie Kick-shawes."

The Englishmen who had never left England tended to look upon Frenchmen as devious and unhygienic, and their food as oily and reeking of garlic. Only an egg in its shell, they said, escapes the contamination.

The Russians agreed. A grand duke who once a

week for six months had enjoyed a roast saddle of lamb *à la provençale* at the Petit Moulin Rouge finally asked Escoffier for the recipe. When he learned that it contained garlic, he announced that he did not understand how *that* could be used in a first-class restaurant.

Shakespeare's Harry Hotspur shared this opinion:

> I had rather live
> With cheese and garlic in a windmill, far,
> Than feed on cates [delicacies] and have him talk
>     to me
> In any summer-house in Christendom.

Fortunately, this attitude did not prevail with those who had traveled abroad. "They order these things better in France," one traveler reported. Some sent their cooks across the Channel, or imported French chefs. Against which venture, Mrs. Hannah Glasse, the cookbook writer, warned: "If gentlemen will have French cooks, they must pay for French tricks."

Rumored extravagance was another source of prejudice. "They reckon on 685 ways of dressing eggs in the French kitchen; we hope our half-dozen recipes give sufficient variety for the English kitchen," wrote Dr. William Kitchiner around 1820 in *The Cook's Oracle.*

The prejudice, it must be admitted, was not all one-sided. When Eleanor of Aquitaine sailed to England to marry Henry Plantagenet in 1154, she brought her cooks along. But unlike the techniques of the Medici chefs, those of Eleanor's cooks left no lasting impression.

Neither, at least among the middle classes, had Carême's.

French visitors complained that an average English dinner consisted of "a piece of half-boiled, or half-roasted, meat; and a few cabbage leaves, boiled in plain water; on which they pour a sauce made of flour and butter, the usual method of dressing vegetables in England.

"They eat at all hours, everywhere and unceasingly . . . The fare of a delicate, ethereal girl would easily still the inner cravings of two Parisian bargees . . ."

Others observed that the English were not "great consumers of fruit and vegetables, and they are right; for both the one and the other with them are very tasteless . . . Salad . . . mostly consists of a lettuce just cut in two . . . Vegetables are simply boiled in water and handed around with the meat."

As recently as the First World War, the American ambassador to Britain observed that only three vegetables were ever served, and two of them were cabbage. Ford Madox Ford praised Provence because Brussels sprouts would not grow there. Peter Kalm, the Scandinavian naturalist, commented in his *Journal* that "the art of cooking as practiced by most Englishmen does not extend much beyond roast beef and plum pudding."

And of their puddings, one bewildered Frenchman

said: "They bake them in an oven, they boil them with meat, they make them fifty several ways."

Even the English themselves were critical. A. V. Kirwan, author of *Host and Guest,* published in 1864, wrote: "Men dine to satisfy hunger in England, and to sustain and strengthen themselves . . . We have given birth to a Bacon, a Locke, a Shakespeare, a Watt; but we are without a Vatel, a Béchamel, or a Carême. We have perfected railroads, steamboats, and canals, but we cannot make a *suprême de volaille* in perfection, nor arrange *des petit choux en profiteroles . . .* We have not yet invented three hundred and sixty-four ways to dress eggs." This egg idea continued to lie in the nests of their minds, although the quantity, by then, was considerably diminished.

The Briton abroad also came under fire, particularly in restaurants. "Englishmen stuff themselves on double portions of meat, order whatever is most costly, drink the headiest wines, and do not always leave without support." What was worse, they were known to bring their own bottled sauces with them.

From the French point of view that was an unforgivable sin, albeit typically British. Britain had adopted ketchup as its own, and gloried in it. "In England, there are sixty different religions, and only one sauce" was the report.

The word is spelled several ways, and there is similar confusion about its origin. Some ketchup researchers say it is derived from the Siamese *kachiap;* others that it comes from the Amoy-Chinese *keôchiap;* still others from the Chinese *kê-tsiap,* these being pickled fish brines. *Kettner's Book of the Table,* however, states that we owe ketchup to the Japanese, that "the true Japanese word is *kitjap.*"

Brillat-Savarin mentions *calchup,* and the *Larousse Gastronomique* offers a recipe for *Ketchup aux champignons,* but it was in Britain that ketchups and their uses really flourished. A whole volume could be filled with nothing but their ketchup recipes.

In *The Cook's Oracle,* Dr. Kitchiner gave his rule for Walnut Catsup, beginning with "Take two hundred walnuts when quite tender," and ending: "By adding a glass of brandy to each quart, it will keep all the better." The good doctor also invented a sauce of shaved lemon peel and brandy which inevitably appears in his book as Pudding Catsup.

But walnuts, mushrooms, and oysters seem to be the chief ingredients of those thick purées which Balzac compared to mashed rose beetles. Tomatoes, the base of the ketchup we know best today, were still regarded with suspicion in the British Isles, even when the "Amorous Apples" were cooked. "To serve a hot tomato by stuffing it with onion, parsley, and shallot is mischievous meddling carried to its highest pitch!" cried one Victorian.

Actually, it was not so much the ingredients of these

sauces that distressed the Continental gastronomes; it was the fact of their constant and indiscriminate use. "If you love GOOD CATSUP, gentle reader," suggests the tireless Dr. Kitchiner, "make it yourself . . . and you will have a delicious Relish for Made dishes, Rag-outs, Soups, Sauces, or Hashes." One might say they even put sauce on sauces.

"Each person seasoned his meat as he pleased with the different sauces which were placed on the tables in bottles of various shapes," a visiting Frenchman summed it up.

And it is still going on. *The Queen Cookery Book*, published in London in 1960, includes a recipe for filets of sole advising the handing around of a *"Sauce Robert Escoffier* which can be bought in bottles."

Even Escoffier, after his London experience, came to agree. In his *Guide Culinaire*, published years later, he admitted that *Sauce Robert Escoffier* "may be bought ready-made," and was "especially suitable for pork, veal, poultry, and even fish." But although he gave his name and part-time efforts to a bottling business, he continued to insist that "a sauce must fit the roast or fish as closely as a tight-fitting skirt fits a woman."

It was at the outposts of the empire that envoys and other travelers within the realm had first acquired the soy-chutney-ketchup taste, and they introduced at home the ones that could most easily be duplicated. Sir Marcus Sandys brought from Bengal to Messrs. Lea and Perrins, chemists in Worcestershire, a mixture his Hindu chefs had served him, and suggested they try to copy it for possible sale.

Mustard was another popular condiment. In medieval times the seeds had been kept in jars with honey or vinegar. Then a housewife in Durham ground her mustard seeds into a paste and "Durham mustard" became an instant craze. Of it, and Messrs. Lea and Perrins', a traveling European wrote: "Their flavour as I can best describe it is that of fireworks which have been thoughtfully set alight in readiness for swallowing."

Some food historians explain the dullness of nineteenth-century British cooking by the stuffy respectability of the Victorian court. The Queen had a German consort; things French did not particularly interest her, in spite of her winters at Menton. In any case, she did not share with her son, the Prince of Wales, a fondness for Continental cuisine. It was, indeed, her constant fear that "Bertie" might turn out to be another Prinny, of whose character she totally disapproved.

What was served at the British court? We have the record of a repast enjoyed by George III and Queen Charlotte in 1762. "On the side table was a large Joynt, for example a large Sirloin of Beef Cold and also a Boars Head and a Sallad; 2nd Course always one Roast, one of pastry and Spinage and Sweetbreads,

Macaron, Scollop and Oysters or the like." Supper featured a "Joynt of Cold Mutton."

"In number of dishes and change of meat," wrote an observer, "the nobility of England (whose cooks are for the most part musical-headed Frenchmen and strangers) do most exceed."

Victoria had a considerable advantage over her ancestors in having an Italian-born, French-educated, "musical-headed" chef named Charles Elme Francatelli, who in 1846 published *The Modern Cook,* since the palate was "as worthy of education as the eye and the ear." This enterprising man must have been hard put to introduce his own Italian and French contributions and still please Her Majesty and Prince Albert with their Germanic-English tastes.

His recipe for "Common Stock for Sauces" called for one hundred and twenty pounds of stewing beef, in addition to lean ham, two legs of white veal, chickens, wild rabbits, and vegetables in comparable amounts. Waste was rampant. For his turtle soup he advised: "Procure a fine, lively turtle," weighing at least one hundred pounds. Turtles were popular at royal dinner parties; so was venison, for which Francatelli was the first we know of to serve melted currant jelly, the forerunner of Cumberland sauce, our usual accompaniment to game.

There is no question that the meals were overlong, overcooked, and oversauced. There was no one like

Francatelli, a pupil of Carême, to take a fresh trout
from the ponds at Windsor and turn it into a mélange
of timbales, quenelles, and mushrooms; or a sturgeon
into a "glutinously rich soup."

He enhanced the "thin Windsor soup" with his *pass-
atelli à la Bolognese,* a pasta-like garnish of bread crumbs
mixed with Parmesan, eggs, and nutmeg, and simmered in a broth of wild chanterelles. For a banquet
for the Chinese ambassador, he ornamented the bouillon with tiger-lily bulbs.

He also had a way with vegetables, drenching them
with double-cream until, as one writer observes, they
were "so completely coated by rich disguises that one
could never know whether he had eaten a turnip or a
truffle." Favorite "dressed vegetables" in the Queen's
household were Brussels sprouts, salsify, and sea kale.

The *pièces montées* of Carême's day persisted with
cakes and pastry in the shapes of castles, dragons, and
heraldic shields. "One feels," fussed a commentator
on the scene, "it was a vandalism to eat any part of the
dish." Francatelli also liked to create, for the amusement of the court, sponge cakes in the shape of roasts
and joints.

There is no denying, however, that beef reigned
supreme. "It ennobled our hearts, and enriched our
blood," wrote the poet Richard Leveridge. Either
Charles II, James I, or Henry VIII (the names tend to
vary in the telling) "being invited to dinner by one of

his nobles, and seeing a large loin of beef at his table, drew out his sword, and in a frolic knighted it."

Alas for legend, the French had long before christened the cut *sur loin* because it lay just above the loin section.

For years any meat had meant beef to a Britisher. A commentary of 1589 records that "biefe of all flesh is most usual among English men." It is reminiscent of the item on a French provincial menu: *bifstek d'agneau* (beefsteak of lamb).

In any case, the roast, whether or not piped into the dining hall to the tune of "The Roast Beef of England," remained the most eagerly awaited offering at the tables of Britain.

Prince Albert had for many years cherished the dream of an international exhibition, a sort of trade fair in which, ideally, the displayed products of many countries would promote understanding and brotherhood and ultimately peace. To provide housing for such an exhibit, Sir Joseph Paxton was engaged. Sir Joseph had designed a huge glass conservatory for the Duke of Devonshire at Chatsworth. Now he supervised the construction in Hyde Park of a tremendous, glittering, three-tiered glass-and-iron building which was immediately dubbed the Crystal Palace. It resembled nothing so much as le Jardin d'Hiver, erected two years earlier in the Champs Elysées, a structure Victor

Hugo had described as "an enormous iron cage, as big as four or five cathedrals, with an immense amount of glass."

Covering eighteen acres, and enclosing three towering elms, the giant greenhouse had London agog. Naturally there were critics: John Ruskin called it "a cucumber frame." But the people flocked to it, among them the Queen herself. Victoria, who had so disapproved of the Royal Pavillion at Brighton that she removed many of its ornaments, had nothing but praise for Albert's Crystal Palace.

To celebrate its opening, a creation called the "Hundred-Guinea Dish" was presented to the Prince and the Lord Mayor of London by the mayors of Great Britain and Ireland. The dish consisted, in part, of: five turtle heads, twenty-four capons, eighteen turkeys, eighteen fatted pullets, ten grouse, twenty pheasants, forty-five partridges, one hundred snipe, three dozen pigeons, six plovers, forty woodcock, three dozen quail, six dozen larks, and an "undisclosed number of ortolans from Belgium." Shades of the old "pyramids"! Garnishes included cockscombs, croustades, crawfish, truffles, mushrooms, American asparagus, *quennelles de volaille,* green mangos, and "a new sauce." Obviously the architect of this structure was not an Englishman; there was no beef at all.

The exhibition was officially opened by the Queen on May Day, 1851, and until mid-October it was thronged with more than six million visitors hoping to catch a glimpse of the Kohinoor diamond or the Queen herself, who continued to drop in several times a week. "The whole period of the Great Exhibition will be remembered with wonder and admiration by all," she noted in her journal.

One facet which was not remembered with any kind of wonder or admiration was the refreshment offered. Schweppes had the concession; raspberry vinegar, spruce and ginger beer, and tea and coffee were the only beverages sold in the three "refreshment rooms." There were Bath buns and Sally Lunn cakes, cold savory pies and Cornish pasties, blancmanges and jellies made from animal hides, and ices which hurt people's teeth.

It is hardly surprising that those who could afford it went next door to Gore House, where a French chef had set up the "Gastronomic Symposium of All Nations." It is also hardly surprising that the chef was the same one who had prepared the "Hundred-Guinea Dish."

Alexis Benôit Soyer was born in 1809 in Meaux-en-Brie, a small town better known for producing the cheese cherished by gourmets since the monks at Reuil-en-Brie taught Charlemagne to eat the crusts in 774. It was decided by Alexis's mother that he should become a priest. But his older brother was a chef in

Paris, and that vocation appealed to Alexis more. At the age of twelve he became an apprentice at Chez Grignon, an establishment of twenty dining rooms in the rue Viviénne, where M. Bailly had had his famous patisserie.

French cooks were in demand in England, irresistible salaries were offered, and in 1831 Soyer went to London. By 1846, the year of Escoffier's birth, he was well known as the brilliant *chef de cuisine* at the Reform Club, an exclusive political *pied-à-terre* celebrated for its "gastronomic perfection" and "matchless culinary arrangements," as *The Spectator* put it. Thackeray, a frequent visitor, claimed that Soyer's chops were the "best in the world." Cutlets Reform still appear on British menus.

The imaginative and resourceful French chef was obviously well qualified to prepare the "Hundred-Guinea Dish," his *Extravagance Culinaire.* It would seem that he should be equally qualified to do well with his "Gastronomic Symposium" at Gore House. Instead, he lost seven thousand pounds and his reputation for success.

What could have gone wrong? There was certainly something for everyone. Besides alcoholic drinks of all sorts, the Russian visitors to the International Exposition were offered caviar; the Persians, sherbet; the Chinese, stewed dog; the Americans, "johnny-cakes and canvas-back ducks." The dining rooms were many and splendid; there was an outdoor Pavilion of All Nations to seat fifteen hundred, in a garden "crammed with choicest roses."

There was a Hall of Architectural Wonders, a Banqueting Bridge, a Transatlantic Antechamber, a Grotto of Eternal Snow, and a Gypsy Dell, complete with fortuneteller.

There was, in fact, much too much. Soyer's biographer, adopting a gastronomic metaphor, admits that the chef had bitten off more than he could chew. Worse than that, there were some influential Victorians who objected to "confused merriment and noise" so close to Albert's exhibition. One, a Mr. Pownall, unfortunately in charge of issuing liquor licenses, paid a surprise visit one evening, and announced to the Middlesex Sessions that he had never seen "a more dangerous place for the morals of young persons . . . or been a witness to such disgraceful dissipation."

It was attitudes such as these that Escoffier and Ritz had to confront when, forty years later, they came to London and D'Oyly Carte's new hotel in the Strand.

Victoria was still on the throne, now in constant mourning. Men still dined at their clubs, those private and sacred retreats of respectability and good food, particularly Crockford's and the Reform, where Soyer's high standards of excellence carried on. In *The Food of London,* published in 1854, George Dodd suggested that "the Battle of Waterloo was in one sense the cause of the present club system. With the cessation of war . . . the officers, accustomed to Mess together when on duty . . . established a Club, mainly in the view of making their slender incomes carry them on as comfortably as might be."

Their wives dined at home. Brillat-Savarin, who never married, wrote that he enjoyed eating with pretty women. Lord Byron, on the other hand, declared that he loathed to see women eat. Disraeli agreed, stating: "If a woman eats she may destroy her spell, and if she will not eat, she destroys our dinner."

Alexis Soyer, as usual, had a flamboyant way of putting it: "Permit me to point out to you, Mylord, that a gastronomical reunion without ladies is in my eyes a garden without flowers, the ocean without its waves, a flotilla without sails." But he never succeeded in introducing women to the Reform Club.

All was not lost at home, though. A flurry of cookbooks, including Soyer's, enabled the ladies to order, and their cooks to prepare, meals almost as good as those served in the clubs. In 1845, Eliza Acton published *Modern Cookery for Private Families.* A poet at heart, she offered recipes for "The King of Oude's Omlet," "Yorkshire Ploughman's Salad," and "Jelly of Siberian Crabs" (wild crab apples). She too deplored that "the daily waste of excellent provisions almost exceeds belief."

Undoubtedly the most enduring cookbook of the time was written by a young woman of twenty-four without, obviously, years of experience in the kitchen. Isabella Beeton's *Book of Household Management* was reprinted in America as recently as 1969. Three inches thick, it contains rules for the Mistress, the Housekeeper, and the Economy of the Kitchen, also the duties of the footman and the coachman, as well as precepts for Victorian manners and morals, and discreet conversation at table.

Why did she feel compelled to compile this opus, lithe little Isabella, who was to die in childbirth before her thirtieth year? "We have frequently been told by brilliant foreign writers, half philosophers, half chefs, that we are the worst cooks on the face of the earth," she wrote in indignation. "Why should the English, as a people, remain more ignorant than their continental neighbours?"

It was exactly this ignorance that Richard D'Oyly Carte sought to remedy in the new hotel he called the Savoy.

It was obviously named for the adjacent theater, but where did *that* name come from? It came from France. In 1246, King Henry III of England presented to the uncle of his Queen, Eleanor of Provence, a stretch of land on the Thames River for the annual rent of three barbed arrows. Upon it Peter, the ninth Count of Savoie, proceeded to erect the "fayrest Mannor in Europe."

Actually, it was more of a palace, "big enough for a large part of an army," and to it were invited scores of influential French noblemen, including Simon de Montfort, and a bevy of "beautiful foreign ladies" to be wed to English titles. King John of Valois, captured by the Black Prince, was held prisoner there; John of Gaunt lived there; Chaucer dined and wrote there.

Then in 1381 the palace was burned, all but the chapel, by Wat Tyler's mob, and remained in ruins for over a century until Henry VII turned part of it into a hospital for the poor. In another section, the second Marquess of Worcester built Worcester House, where, one September midnight in 1660, the Duke of York, later King James II and father of two queens, was secretly married.

Georges Auguste Escoffier was forty-three when he came to England. He spoke no English and did not attempt to learn. If he spoke as they spoke, he once explained, he might begin to cook as they cooked.

Many things distressed him. The British custom of high, or cream, teas with jelly and jam, sugared buns, cakes, pastries, and other sweets was bound to spoil their appetites for dinner. Even worse was the American habit, now spreading, of *le cocktail,* not to mention the ice water with their meals. And the electric kitchen had obviously not been designed with him in mind; he continued to cook over coal or wood-burning stoves.

The highly praised electricity in the dining room was too bright, and therefore unflattering to the ladies he hoped to woo to his tables. Although refined Victorian women still did not dine out in public, Escoffier, who enjoyed creating dishes for them, almost single-handedly changed that attitude by planning with Ritz the after-theater suppers that D'Oyly Carte had envisioned.

To his Savoy Restaurant, as it was called, with its softly shaded lamps and fresh flowers from Covent Garden, ladies at last began to come. They found the cuisine delicate and beautiful to look upon, and the setting exquisite.

From time to time the Prince of Wales brought his women friends: Lily Langtry, Lady Dudley, Lady Randolph Churchill, the Countess de Grey. One afternoon he called Ritz with a request that Escoffier produce a surprise for an intimate theater supper. "You know what I like. Arrange a dinner to my taste." Escoffier invented, prepared, and presented to them a dish which he called *les cuisses de nymphes à l'aurore,* "the thighs of nymphs at dawn."

The Prince's guests enjoyed the uniquely flavored and tinted light meat in a pale pinkish-gold *chaud-froid* surrounded by sprigs of tarragon. But what was it? Nobody knew, and, in the presence of the Prince, no one dared ask.

The next morning a second call came from Marlborough House. His Royal Highness desired the recipe for M. Escoffier's *cuisses de nymphes.* In answer to the
command, Auguste had to reveal that what the party
had supped upon was frogs' legs in a paprika-shaded
wine sauce to resemble the dawn; the tarragon por-
trayed seaweed.

Neither the Prince of Wales, nor indeed any self-
respecting Englishman, had ever before eaten a frog or
any part of one, let alone an imitation of seaweed.
What was to be done? If Escoffier cherished momentary hopes of being returned to France, they were soon
dashed. *Les cuisses de nymphes à l'aurore* became one of
Albert Edward's favorites; it appeared regularly on the
restaurant's menu; every snob in London was ordering
it. And Escoffier came to be known as the man who
taught the British to eat frogs.

Shortly after the Savoy opened, an Australian singer
who called herself Nellie Melba moved in, largely
because of Escoffier, whom she had known in Paris. It
is a temptation, for both their sakes, to call her "the
toast of London." For she was the reigning soprano at
Covent Garden, the sublime heroine of Italian opera.

But Wagner was the current rage; it was fashionable
to attend, if not necessarily to like or understand, his
operas; and Nellie was determined to sing Wagner.
Although she knew that she lacked the voice for it, and
the critics realized it too, she insisted on performing

the role of Elsa in *Lohengrin.* To bring good luck, she sent a box-seat ticket to Escoffier for opening night.

The next evening she entertained some friends at supper. She knew that she had not achieved a great success, but she had had her way, and the critics had been kind enough. Planning the dessert, and unable to decide between ice cream, which she craved, and fruit, which she felt she ought to eat instead, she compromised and ordered Escoffier to flame peaches over ice cream.

But Escoffier felt that a totally cold dish was more harmonious with the rest of the menu, and thereby achieved for his client a kind of universal immortality that her operatic roles never did. He placed poached fresh peaches over vanilla ice cream and coated the whole with a glaze of strawberry jam. Actually, this was just the first version of the famous dessert. Escoffier was never completely satisfied with that combination of flavors, and eventually substituted a raspberry purée.

In any case, it was the presentation of the dish that made it spectacular. To express his gratitude for the ticket and his general admiration of the lady, he set the dessert between the wings of a *Lohengrin* swan carved out of ice. On a nest of spun sugar and strawberry leaves it was wheeled to Nellie's table. Its name was *les pêches au cygne.*

*Pêches Melba* came later at the opening of another great hotel.

Melba toast was originally *toast Marie.* As was his custom, Escoffier was spending Sunday with the Ritzes at their rambling "country house" in Golders Green. The children, Charles and René, were playing on the lawn with a pair of Newfoundland dogs, while their mother posed for endless experiments with lighting. Ritz and Escoffier were trying to find the kind of lighting most complimentary to the complexions, jewels, and gowns of women guests at the Savoy.

During tea time in their garden, Mme Ritz expressed a wish that toast could be thinner. Escoffier made a trip to the pantry and returned with crisp, curling pieces of toast that he had achieved by barely toasting the bread, then splitting it through into two slices and returning them to the oven. *"Voilà, toast Marie!"* he said.

But Marie Louise was modest. "That is too anonymous," she protested. When Nellie Melba, on a diet, discovered Escoffier's thin toast, she graciously allowed *her* name to be attached to it. Ironically, Nellie's slimming efforts only served to make her look older.

Auguste continued to create dishes for his friend: *poires Melba,* also with vanilla ice cream; *coupe Melba,* peaches filled with almond praline on ice cream covered with a veil of spun sugar; and one of her particular favorites, plovers' eggs *en croûte* with caviar, which Escoffier called "undoubtedly the richest and most delicate of hors d'oeuvres."

*Poularde Tosca* is generally supposed to have been

named in honor of Melba's role in the Puccini opera. But Melba never sang *Tosca*. It is conceded that the poached stuffed chicken with white sauce, celery, and truffles was dedicated to another dear friend, Sarah Bernhardt, opening in Paris in 1887 as the heroine of Sardou's play *La Tosca*.

Before the arrival of Escoffier, Sarah said of the Savoy that "the menu was medieval." Now she agreed with her actor colleague Coquelin and others that London was at last fit to live in.

For Melba's rival, eighteen-years-older Adelina Patti, Escoffier also prepared a poached stuffed chicken: this version with rice and *sauce suprême,* garnished with asparagus tips, truffles, and artichoke bottoms. *Coupe Adelina Patti* was vanilla ice cream topped with *crème Chantilly* and surrounded by brandied cherries.

Emma Calvé, another diva, was honored with a coupe of white cherries, currant jelly, ice cream, and *crème Chantilly* flavored with raspberries.

*Poires Mary Garden* consisted in part of pears and cherries in a claret syrup thickened with "raspberry-flavored red currant jelly." Dame Nellie expressed gratification that this concoction never achieved the acclaim of the dishes named for *her.*

One of the guests at the after-opera party where *les pêches au cygne* had been unveiled was Louis Philippe

Robert, fourteenth Duke of Orleans and the Bourbon Pretender to the throne of France. A close friend of Melba's, he often dined with her at the Savoy on lobster and champagne, and is said to have had an extraordinary effect upon her singing. George Bernard Shaw found her "transfigured" by him.

Oldest son of the Comte de Paris, elegant, educated, and entertaining, he was living in exile in England. His being there was a bit of an embarrassment to the Victorian court, and his pet lion cubs terrified the staff of the hotel, but César Ritz and Auguste Escoffier were delighted to serve him. Ritz ordered for his apartment at the Savoy a complete dinner service of Vallauris porcelain, French blue with the royal fleur-de-lis in gold. And Escoffier contrived dish after dish to please him.

"What feats of ingenuity have we not been forced to perform," he wrote later, "in order to meet our customers' wishes . . . I have ceased counting the nights spent in the attempt to discover new combinations."

There was more, much more to come.

The Duke of Orleans's sister, Hélène, who had formerly been engaged to Prince Eddy, oldest son of the Prince of Wales, was soon to be married to the Duke of Aosta. She was planning her wedding reception, which, of course, must be held at the Savoy. There was, however, one insurmountable obstacle. The date and the banqueting room had already been spoken for by the Guards Club at whose luncheon the guest of honor would be none other than the Prince of Wales.

The Young Pretender refused to change either the date or the place. It appeared he had already issued the invitations. What was to be done? Calm and contained as always, Ritz suggested that to accommodate the expected throng a few partition walls might be knocked out of the hotel's basement.

"What!" cried the Comtesse de Paris. "Ritz intends putting them down in the cellars? Not to be thought of!" And Louis Philippe Robert reacted with comparable horror.

But Ritz was recalling the time, years before, when he had transformed a restaurant in Baden-Baden into a "woodland scene." It was, in fact, the very reason for his being at the Savoy now.

The dividing walls in the storage and billiard rooms were removed; green and silver paint was applied in elegant design. Mirrors and frosted glass lent an airy look and an illusion of coolness. Leafy trees stood in vine-twined tubs; ferns and wildflowers sprang from moss in vases carved of ice. La France roses, iris, lilies, and other fleur-de-lis symbols abounded.

In this fairyland setting the wedding reception of the Duke of Aosta and Hélène of Orleans took place on the twenty-third of June 1895. The menu card showed a crown above an oval containing three fleur-de-lis. It also showed a ten-course spread including *velouté à l'Italienne,* for Aosta; *truite saumonée royale; soufflé d'é-*

*crevisses à la Florentine,* a Medici contribution; *salade Alexandra;* and *pêches Princesse,* with red and white rose petals, in honor of the Princess, who was fond of Hélène and would not miss her wedding celebration. There were also nectarines on miniature fruit trees, to be cut off the branches with tiny gold scissors, party favors.

Escoffier's own copy of the menu was signed by many of the royal guests: Arthur, Duke of Connaught, the Prince of Wales's younger brother; Albert de Belgique, later King Albert I of Belgium; and the Princess Beatrice, Victoria's daughter.

When Princess Alexandra showed her menu to her husband, who had formerly declared that he was glad he had the excuse of the Guards luncheon not to have to eat in the cellar, he "mourned over it."

One might have expected to find the dessert to be *poires Belle Hélène* as a compliment to the bride. But these cold poached pears on vanilla ice cream served with hot chocolate sauce had been named for the heroine of Offenbach's popular operetta about Helen of Troy, *La Belle Hélène,* whose star, Hortense Schneider, was an early and much-publicized lady friend of the Prince of Wales. With typical sensitivity, Escoffier did not risk an affront or embarrassment to Alexandra.

When he did prepare it, though, perhaps with the memory of another Hélène in a garden, he added violets and called it simply *poires Hélène.*

His other *Hélène* desserts have violets too, crystallized or pralined; his *coupe Hélène, charlotte Hélène,* and *meringues glacées Hélène* are strewn with these candied flowers. Dame Nellie Melba, who considered the role of Violetta in *La Traviata* her "special property," also considered violets on her ices a particular tribute to her.

Years later, when the *Mona Lisa,* on loan from the Louvre, was exhibited at the National Gallery in Washington, *poires Hélène* were served at the reception. Though the name was changed to "Pears *Mona Lisa,*" the recipe, provided by Mme Lucat, wife of the French ambassador, was basically the same, and the dish was decorated with a "crown of fresh flowers to improve the aspect."

Looking back on the Savoy days, Mme Ritz wrote that in a few months it became clear that the hotel's success was spectacular. The restaurant became the meeting place nightly of the cream of society and the most brilliant stars of the theatrical firmament: Bernhardt, Henry Irving, Ellen Terry, Beerbohm Tree, and Oscar Wilde, who said that after a good dinner one could forgive anybody, even one's own relatives.

There were world-famous singers from Covent Garden: the de Reszke brothers, Adelina Patti, Melba; and the "professional beauties" forming the Marlborough House circle.

"All of these found at the Savoy the delicate fare and

atmosphere which they sought. Gradually those who had never been seen dining in public restaurants abandoned their clubs, preferring to spend their evenings at the Savoy, where they could count upon the collaboration of the most refined of chefs and the most famous hotelier in the whole world.''

In private dining rooms, named for Gilbert and Sullivan operettas—*Patience, Pinafore, Mikado, Iolanthe*—the great hostesses of London and the Counties presided at dinner parties. Sometimes they would gather with their guests in a secluded corner of the restaurant where Ritz would place his famous RESERVED card along with their favorite flowers.

Puccini entertained Melba there. Sir Henry Irving moved into a suite. Mark Twain came to feast upon baked apple, Melba toast, and ale, while dreaming of Missouri buckwheat cakes and milk. Lily Langtry is rumored to have dropped a sliver of ice down the back of the Prince of Wales.

Bernhardt would hurry back from a performance so that Escoffier could prepare her favorite *zephyr de poularde,* sliced breast of pullet on foie gras with truffles and asparagus tips. As a special treat on her birthdays, this old friend from the Petit Moulin Rouge would come to her suite to make scrambled eggs, which she swore she could never enjoy so much elsewhere. He assured her that the secret lay in the silver omelet pan which he had brought with him from France. She despised garlic, so she never knew that on the prongs of the fork with which Auguste stirred her inimitable eggs he had impaled a clove of garlic.

Perfection remained César Ritz's password. Ladies in the restaurant for dinner must wear full evening dress "and no hats" and be accompanied by gentlemen in formal attire. Flowers must be fresh, delicate, and not overly fragrant, tablecloths and napkins embroidered, Christofle silver gleaming, Baccarat crystal washed in lemon water before polishing, and wine properly advised.

The behavior and appearance of his staff were constantly supervised. To ensure fresh rolls on weekends, a baker was imported from Vienna; for music no one less than Johann Strauss, Jr., was engaged. When Escoffier worried that the waltzes might distract attention from his entrées, Ritz reassured him that the romantic mood induced would encourage his clients to linger longer, enjoying another pastry or savory, while ordering one further bottle of champagne. "Ask the sommelier," he added.

"The Savoy," wrote an appreciative observer, "became the sacrosanct meeting place of international aristocracy, an oasis for artists, the mecca of gourmets, and a goal of pilgrimages from the five parts of the world . . . It transcended geographical boundaries and became a free territory of France."

The old Comte de Savoie would have been pleased.

What happened to the idyll? There are various accounts. Some say Ritz had insoluble differences with his board of directors; some say he became autocratic; others tell the story of his being involved in a dispute over a housekeeper of whom he disapproved. "He would come home depressed," his wife remembered, "by some manoeuvre of hers."

In any case, it was only natural for him to desire a hotel of his own. He must have felt that he had done all he could for D'Oyly Carte. He had left him with the greatest establishment in the world.

When Ritz departed in 1897, Escoffier went with him. So did much of their clientele. "Where they go, we shall follow," thundered the Prince of Wales in his German accent. Fortunately for the Marlborough House set, in a few years they had to go only as far as the Haymarket and Pall Mall.

# 5

★ ★ ★ ★

# THE RITZ

*"He gives nothing who does not give himself."*
*Old French Proverb*

Just as Georges Auguste Escoffier had longed to open
his own restaurant, and had rejoiced in his Faisan Doré
in those sunlit days in Cannes before César Ritz had
appeared on his doorstep, so Ritz had dreams of his
own hotel. Free at last from the demands of the Savoy,
he turned his thoughts back to the Riviera.

There was no doubt that he could go anywhere on
earth he wished. His success in London, as well as
elsewhere, had established him as just what Mme Ritz
had declared: "the most famous hotelier in the whole
world." It was simply up to him to decide where he
was needed, and he could count on financial backing.

Naturally he discussed this with Escoffier, and they
agreed that the south of France, a section that they
both knew well and that was popular with their clients,
might be ideal. But Escoffier had another thought—
Paris. He had never forgotten his days at the Petit
Moulin Rouge of M. Bardoux.

Unexpectedly, the Prince of Wales, who might logically have urged them to stay in London, concurred. He traveled to Paris frequently, and complained that there was not one "decent" hotel there. At the Bristol, where he had stopped for years, his bath consisted of tanks of hot water and a large tub carried into his bedroom.

Bankers, and others who did business in the City of London and had to cross the Channel from time to time, agreed. The lack of bathrooms was certainly the greatest fault. "Furthermore," continued the Prince, "you can take your ease; you will not have to educate Parisian tastes."

Taking their ease was the furthest thought from the minds of Ritz and Escoffier. But the Prince was insistent, and the backers were promising, and Ritz agreed to take a trip to Paris to look over the possibilities.

The life-long love affair between the Prince of Wales and France had begun when he was fourteen years old, accompanying his parents on a state visit to the court of Napoleon III. To the Emperor, and the Empress Eugénie, the slim handsome boy in his kilts remarked upon leaving, "You have a nice country. I should like to stay here and be your son." What Victoria thought of this, or said afterward, we can only imagine, but it was the first of Bertie's many protests against the Victorianism of the Britain he was forced to live in.

Later, as a young man, he traveled often to the Continent, and came to feel at home in Paris, "learning how to be king," as he explained to his mother when she questioned him. Had she entrusted him, as she should have, with the handling of some of the affairs of state, or at least permitted his familiarity with them, he would surely not have felt so bored, restless, and frustrated in England. But the Queen could never overcome the belief that he was responsible for his father's death, caused, as she claimed, from pneumonia caught while visiting the Prince at Cambridge, even though the doctors blamed the defective drains at Windsor Castle for what *they* diagnosed as typhoid fever.

In any case, whether she kept the reins of government from his hands to punish him, or because she did not think he was either very bright or very discreet (as has been rumored), is not really important. The explanation of what so many of his critics have condemned as frivolous, insouciant, and even wicked behavior seems to be that an existence of opening exhibitions and fairs, unveiling art, and presiding at banquets and other ceremonies was not the kind of life for a robust young man with his background and abilities.

The social life at Buckingham Palace was equally dull. The Queen's royal set was confined mostly to the old English nobility and relatives from Europe. And after Albert's death there was little social life, if any. It had been a great relief to the Prince upon his marriage to be able to move into Marlborough House, where he could entertain his own wide circle of friends. Even at a distance, these were frowned upon by his mother; she simply could not understand his liking for industrialists, Americans, and untitled Jews.

The period in France toward the end of the last century is sometimes called *La Belle Époque*. Visitors from around the globe flocked to enjoy its ambience. "England built London for its own use," wrote Emerson, "but France built Paris for the world." César Ritz could not have chosen a more propitious time to plan a hotel there.

He called it *"une petite maison à laquelle je suis très fier de voir mon nom attaché"* ("a little house to which I am very proud to see my name attached"). Actually, the handsome Mansard-built mansion at 15, Place Vendôme, adjoining the Ministry of Justice, had once been the palace of the Duc de Lauzun when the Place was *"des Conquêtes."* Ritz, on his scouting mission, immediately saw the possibilities and reported back to London. Presumably not much was said about the fact that the Place Vendôme had been neglected for years, and that weeds grew among the cobblestones. But the column of the Grand Armée, celebrating Napoleon's victories, which had been pulled down after the Siege of Paris, had been restored.

An English company, headed by Earl Grey, the

Baron de Guinzbourg, and other members of the Prince of Wales's set, helped to finance the venture. When some regretted an apparent lack of room for expansion, Ritz insisted that he did not desire a "grand hotel, only a small, intimate, exclusive work of art."

Further funds were contributed by the Établissements Marnier Lapostolle, creators of the orange-scented, brandy-based French liqueur, Grand Marnier, which Ritz had made popular at the Savoy, and had indeed named.

How does one transform an antique palace into a modern hotel? When Ritz called the place his "little house," he meant it to be a place where his guests could feel at home. He was not unaware for a moment that "home" to many of them was a castle or a manor. Fontainebleau, Versailles, Carnavalet, and the Louvre were studied and sketched for interior designs; fabrics and ornaments were copied; inspiration ran rampant.

Ritz's first undertaking was to clear away the clutter. Having observed patients in Swiss mountaintop sanatoriums, he recognized the hazards of dust. Even at the Savoy, where the advertisements had extolled the "artistic furniture," he had had most of it replaced. Heavily upholstered chairs and sofas, trailing velvet curtains, flocked wallpaper, and ball fringe, however opulent the appearance, were, he felt, definitely unhealthy. At his new hotel the walls were painted; the draperies were light and airy; the furniture had more wood and less horsehair, although the pillows were deep and satiny; and the beds and valances were hung with filmy materials, with Venetian-lace counterpanes. Everything must be washable and washed often.

Light bulbs were painted a delicate peach to give a soft glow; in gilded candelabra, small electric candles (so there would be no smoke) gleamed behind pleated apricot silk shades. As at the Savoy, the food must be properly illumined, but the diners' faces must be romantically flattered. Marie Louise posed again, and the result was indirect lighting, bulbs in alabaster bowls, an innovation for the time.

César Ritz remained a demanding perfectionist, and nowhere more than in this hotel, which was not only to bear his name but also, he sensed, become his monument. "I know what I need for perfect efficiency and elegance in the hotel I want," he stated. His first requirements were that it be "hygienic, efficient, and beautiful," in that order.

Ritz's dream was to present to his clientele "all the refinements of living that a prince might hope to incorporate in his town house." Complete with garden, one might add. Where Escoffier deeply loved flowers, Ritz recognized their aesthetic appeal; he always insisted that his hotels have gardens. Charles Mewès, "a man of taste and understanding" and the architect, fortunately agreed.

As the opening drew near, César and Marie Louise

Ritz checked and rechecked every detail. Nothing that pertained to their guests' comfort was left to chance; no luxurious touch was omitted. "I settled down with almost sensual pleasure to the selection of the linen," Mme Ritz remembers.

It was the same everywhere. Since his Monte Carlo days, Ritz had known that the ultimate success of a hotel depended on its cuisine. He gave Escoffier a free rein, and, one may suppose, whatever he asked for his kitchens.

A great chef is often anything but a great organizer. Happily for Ritz, his friend not only knew exactly what he wanted; he had the tact and perseverance to obtain it. For he too remembered other days: the heat and noise at the Petit Moulin Rouge, the gloom and darkness of the Grand, and the general filth of both. Like Ritz, he deplored the unhygienic atmosphere of most public places.

Kitchens, he insisted, did not have to be chaotic and messy. He planned windows whenever possible, and sufficient overhead lighting. He organized his stoves, ice boxes, counters, and tables so that they were in logical progression, and he also organized his chefs. He recalled all too well the tempers and temperaments of the crew under Ulysse Rohan, the tricks and the jealousies.

Under Escoffier, each man would have a specific duty, and the preparation of a dish would move smoothly and speedily from one to another. The example most often cited is of *oeufs Meyerbeer,* which formerly took fifteen minutes to prepare. In Escoffier's kitchen an *entremetteur* baked the eggs, a *rôtisseur* grilled the kidneys, and a *saucier* prepared the truffle sauce. And there may well have been someone posted by the door to make sure the plates were properly garnished and hot.

Auguste expected his chefs to work hard, and he worked hard himself.

The most surprising innovation, at least to the reporters who came to inspect the hotel before the opening, was not an innovation at all. They were astonished to find old-fashioned wood-and-coal-burning stoves. With electricity everywhere else, how could the stoves have been overlooked? Even gas might have been used.

Auguste pointed out the only gas in the kitchen; it was a ring to keep *le feu éternel,* a boiling-water device for his copper marmite of beef stock, "without which no good cooking can be achieved." Aside from that, he had always cooked over "natural" heat and he intended to continue to do so.

And where were the new enamel and aluminum pots and pans? Patiently Escoffier explained that those were useful in kitchens where labor was wanting, but that was not a problem here. He would use the iron, earthenware, and copper utensils of his mother's kitchen, and of his own kitchens in Nice, Paris, Cannes, Monte Carlo, London, and the fields of Metz.

The Ritz opened on a warm evening in June 1898. It had been raining off and on, but Marie Louise had not stood at the window with a long face. She was far too busy making a final check on light bulbs, hangers in closets, scented soap in the marble bathrooms, and flowers everywhere. She was also worried about her husband. He had been working without ceasing since the property was acquired. Although he had not complained of being tired, he was understandably nervous. And he ate so little: a bit of vegetable soup and some fruit. Still, he was excited and happy, and only laughed when his wife and Auguste tried to tempt him with *truite à la meunière* or *tournedos Rossini*.

Now, elegantly dressed and with his constant carnation, "the whitest and freshest ever seen," he waited in the hall to welcome his guests. He did not believe in large impressive lobbies, feeling that they encouraged loitering. So through the tall windows of his intimate foyer he watched the line of carriages approach over the glistening cobblestones of the Place Vendôme.

Whom did the carriages carry? According to Marie Louise, who stood at the top of the stairs watching with her two young sons, *"Tout Paris."*

"All Paris" consisted, in part, of Marcel Proust,

Sarah Bernhardt, Constant Coquelin, Victorien Sardou, Emile Winter, Baron Pfyffer, Boni de Castellane, Paris Singer, Alberto Santos-Dumont, and members of the Murat, Breteuil, and Rothschild families. From England came the Dukes and Duchesses of Marlborough, Portland, Sutherland, and Norfolk, "The Prince's Set," as they were called in France; from America, Goulds, Vanderbilts, and Drexels.

One cannot help thinking of the Prince of Wales and how he must have missed being there. But Franco-British relations were at a low ebb because of ill feeling over the Boer War, and Victoria had deemed it best that Bertie remain on her side of the Channel.

Had he been allowed to attend, there is no doubt that he would have been as entranced as everyone with all he saw. The light attractive furnishings harmonized with the interiors; the interiors harmonized with the architecture; the architecture with the landscape: all the eye looked upon was harmonious.

The soft, shaded lighting, the profusion of blossoms, the gently falling draperies, the antique mirrors, the luminous garden: how could the effect fail to please? Only *Truth* magazine suggested that "the buffets were perhaps too heavily garlanded with choice flowers."

In the Regency Room, armchairs had been introduced to ensure the comfort of the diners, while lamps concealed in alabaster urns cast their glow toward the ornamented pastel ceilings. The salon reflected the dreams of one man who was already the most celebrated chef in the world, and of another who, upon entering St. Peter's Cathedral for the first time, visualized it as a banquet room.

The opening has been described in one word: "triumphant." "They came! They came!" cried Mme Ritz. And yet, up to the last minute, César had worried that they might not remember, with so much going on in Paris.

What was going on in Paris was that the city, a sudden fountainhead of expression and ideas, was enjoying a kind of renascence. Some called it an "Athenian period." The writers Anatole France, Rostand, Loti, Zola, Verne, were making, or had already made, their marks. Dumas *fils* had recently died, but his plays remained popular. The Impressionists were painting: Manet, Monet, Cézanne, Renoir, Toulouse-Lautrec. Music and musicians were everywhere; the Variétés, Comédie Française, and other theaters were thronged. Paris was a city of art and music.

These combined at Le Moulin Rouge, where Toulouse-Lautrec painted posters of the cabaret stars: Jane Avril, Yvette Guilbert, and La Goulue. Louise Weber, reigning queen of Montmartre, whose stage name translates into "the Glutton," was an uninhibited dancer with red or black silk stockings and a fringe of blond hair. Her welcoming cry of " 'Allo there, Wales!" when the Prince entered Le Jardin de Paris the night of the Grand Prix won her a magnum of champagne from His Royal Highness. And it was Toulouse-Lautrec's poster of La Goulue as she danced her *quadrille réaliste* that brought him his first recognition.

Another popular meeting place was Maxim's in the rue Royale. Although the founder, Maxime Gaillard, died in 1895, shortly after its inauguration, it became a stylish rendezvous with its *sang-rouge* curtains and carpets and its Tiffany glass roof, attracting celebrities from the theater and other arts, aristocrats, and many of the crowned heads of Europe. "It's marvelous," remarked the Prince of Wales; "here, everyone knows me but no one notices me."

One of those he was "not noticed" with was La Belle Otéro, a Spanish gypsy dancer who bathed in the whites of eggs and champagne, and whom the Kaiser called "my little savage." The Baron Ollstreder presented her with Marie Antoinette's diamond *rivière.* Upon another occasion she recovered a diamond brooch offered to her in a soufflé covered with roses. For this *belle,* Escoffier created *les filets de soles Otéro,* in which the poached filets are placed on a bed of shrimp in white wine sauce inside a baked-potato shell, which is then topped with Mornay sauce, glazed quickly, and served on a napkin!

Other patrons included Emilienne d'Alençon, King Leopold of Belgium's favorite soubrette; Gaby Deslys, who performed with two pink rabbits and was the mistress of Portugal's King Manuel; and Liane de Pougy, Napoleon III's guardsman's daughter, who timed her opening night at Les Folies Bergère to coincide with one of the Prince of Wales's visits to Paris, and sent him an invitation. He went. Later she married the Prince of Roumania.

Thus the demimondaines and *grandes cocottes* mingled and dined with the royal and the wealthy in that *fin de siècle* world of French café life when the Ritz began.

All interest was not turned indoors, however. There was horse racing at Longchamps where, in the restaurant of the exclusive Jockey Club, Jules Gouffé, a pupil and disciple of Carême, had once presided. Author of *Le Livre de Cuisine* and other classic cookbooks, Gouffé agreed with his master that service *à la russe* "tends to destroy the tasteful and rich appearance which formerly characterized high-class cookery."

There were also polo and football matches, and bicycle races. Hunting and riding, even falconry, were popular. Automobiles had come onto the scene and were greeted with excitement and wonder. Even more exciting and wonderful were the balloons.

Leader of the ballooning set was Alberto Santos-Dumont, son of "the richest planter in Brazil." On his eighteenth birthday his father sent him to Paris to "see if you can make a man of yourself." Alberto gladly accepted this challenge, and took to the air in a free-sailing silk balloon, reminiscent of the one in which the Divine Sarah had indulged in her famous ride.

No one less than his friend Escoffier packed the lunch for his first aerial trip from Le Jardin d'Acclimation: cold roast beef, sliced chicken, ice cream, petit fours, champagne, coffee, and "a good Chartreuse." Afterward, at the Jockey Club, in his pin-stripe suit, high collar, and derby, Santos-Dumont described Paris as seen from above the treetops, and also his *pique-nique* in the sky. "No dining room is as well decorated," he declared, though certainly not in the presence of César Ritz.

There is no question that as director of the Ritz kitchens and supervisor of the hotel menus, Escoffier changed the tastes and habits of his diners. As recently as two years earlier, a banquet honoring Sarah Bernhardt had been held in the Salle du Zodiac at what was then Paris's grandest hotel, the Grand. It was called her "Day of Glorification," and was no surprise to her, since she had consulted Escoffier in London about the menu. The repast included Ostende oysters, cold salmon-on-trout, *pré-salé* lamb (that lovely meat of the sheep that browse on the absinthe-mixed vegetation of the coastal salt meadows), pullets *à la Sardou,* truffled pheasants, *pâté de foie gras Grand Hôtel, gâteaux Sarah,* and *bombe Tosca.*

This feast might not seem so remarkable were it not for the fact that it was served at noon, and before a matinée. Nevertheless, five hundred admirers, in full evening dress, enjoyed *La Journée Sarah Bernhardt.*

Escoffier was as aware as anyone else, perhaps more, that times were changing. The days of huge meals were coming to an end. People were more conscious of their health, and also of their time. In Brillat-Savarin's day a respectable dinner used to take at least four hours to savor; Escoffier believed that an equally elegant one could be enjoyed in two.

Although he once modestly wrote, "It would be absurd to aspire to fix the destinies of an art," he must have been conscious of the impact of his philosophy upon the Regency Room of the Ritz. *"Faites Simple"* was his motto, and it might just as well have been emblazoned beneath the lion's head and crown on the menu's crest.

And although he acknowledged that the true classic cuisine was born in Carême's kitchens, he understood that modifications were not only inevitable but also advisable. His response to Carême's excesses was a stunning simplicity.

The very word "restaurant" means "restorative." A restaurateur is a restorer. As originally envisioned and practiced in 1765 by a certain M. Boulanger (not a baker), it was a sort of soup kitchen. In the rue Bailleul, under a sign which proclaimed BOULANGER SELLS MAGICAL RESTORATIVES, he served nourishing soups.

Before that, travelers dined in inns at definitely set

times and from definitely set menus. It was a welcome change to be able to drop in at M. Boulanger's whenever hungry and have a choice of his hearty specialties.

The word "soup" does not, as some suppose, derive from the word "supper," nor is it the other way around. A "sop" was a piece of bread soaked in milk or wine before being eaten. The French *soupe* originally meant the crouton in a broth. Now it has come to describe a thick, peasant-style soup containing vegetables and bread, whereas the more usual *potage* indicates something more refined.

One day the enterprising Boulanger decided to enhance his menu by offering sheep's feet in a bowl of white sauce. Although the innkeepers protested that this was indeed a ragout, or stew, which he had no license to sell, an understanding Parliament decreed that it was not, and the dish attained instant notoriety. It was even served at Versailles to Louis XV, who did not like it at all.

From such humble beginnings did the "restaurant" spring. It was both Escoffier's and Ritz's desire to return to it some part of its original simplicity and restorative quality.

No one was more in need of this than their old friend the Prince of Wales.

He was still at the university when he began to show symptoms of a disease for which there was no known cure: compulsive eating. The known *cause* seemed to be lack of affection at home, and yet when he wanted to go fox hunting, his parents forbade it for fear he would break his neck. So he was deprived of exercise as well.

By the time he was thirty, he was definitely overweight. To try to control this, his doctors, instead of putting him on a diet, sent him to Baden-Baden and Marienbad for "the cure." This annual event, with its unpleasant-tasting spring water, its long walks (a mile between each spring), its boiled food, its mud treatments, and its early risings and bedtimes, must have been a real hardship for His Royal Highness, and upon his return to England three weeks later he would put the whole thing out of his mind and his regime.

When he became so portly that he could no longer fasten the bottom button on his vest, he started a fashion.

Of course it was next to impossible to be a much-entertained prince and also weight-conscious. Hostesses, both political and intimate, vied with one another to provide the most groaning of boards at their weekend houseparties in the country.

Breakfast became a many-course affair with roast ptarmigan, chops and sausages, kidneys and kippers, mushrooms, porridge, and a cold buffet of York ham, tongue, and wild game. Only a few hours later was "elevenses," with Bertie's favorite gingerbread and ginger liqueur.

Lunch ran to at least five courses, with terrines of quail, fish from local streams, cutlets and steaks, galantine of chicken and young wild rabbit, cold pigeon pies with the little claws sticking up through the crust, and greengage sherbets to renew the appetite as plates and platters were changed. Sometimes there would be a "shooting luncheon," with ladies, footmen, and hampers arriving in the field in carriages, and tents and tables set up.

Tea, as a bulwark of British life, would offer the inevitable tiered trays of watercress, bloater paste, tomato, and cucumber sandwiches; crumpets and scones; damson fool, gooseberry queen, lemon curd, Bath buns, bramble jelly, and Shrewsbury cakes.

Dinners were lengthy and elaborate, running to as many as fourteen courses, and as French as possible, whether the chefs were from Glasgow or Moscow. "Those meals!" remembered Vita Sackville-West. "Those endless, extravagant meals, in which they all indulged . . . The servants came and went, handing dishes and pouring wine in the light of many candles . . . among the bowls of grapes and peaches."

And to please His Royal Highness a champagne supper was served at midnight. It might include anchovy cheese, potted shrimps, rabbit-brain pâté, and trifle or tipsy parson. And always in his bedroom he would expect to find a plate of cold lobster patties, a salmis of whatever game had been bagged on the shoot, and a noble Stilton, Double Gloucester, or Wensleydale.

Entertaining the Prince of Wales and his entourage for a hunting weekend, or whatever, proved to be a rather expensive do, and many of the old County families found themselves unable to compete with the nouveau riche, which often included Jews and Americans. The Prince did not care. He continued to go where the women were beautiful and amusing, and the food excellent and plentiful.

By the time the Savoy was inaugurated, the Prince of Wales was forty-eight and in danger of destroying his health with his gigantic meals. When the Ritz opened in 1898, those who knew him well called him "Tum-Tum" and were seriously worried about him. And yet his energies seemed as undiminished as his appetite. He sent word to his friends across the Channel that the old Carlton House in the Haymarket was to be remodeled and rebuilt as a new hotel. Would they come?

This time it was Marie Louise Ritz who demurred. Why should they leave Paris, where they were so happy and enjoying such success? Five o'clock tea in the "palm garden" had already become a tradition. Families who had never dined out together in public reserved tables in the Regency Room for their Sunday *déjeuner.* And had not Boni de Castellane threatened to dismiss his chef because it was folly to try to compete with Escoffier?

Our guests depend on us, said Marie Louise. Among these was Marcel Proust, who preferred the Ritz because "no one jostled him there." Frail and aloof, his coat collar turned up, his pockets jammed with books, he sat in his customary corner eating chocolate ice cream and *petites madeleines,* and drinking green tea. Once he told a friend that he had a vast amount of table silver which he never used because he ate at the Ritz. And when he did not feel like going out he would call Escoffier to send over a roast chicken.

Behind Mme Ritz's objections was her continued concern for her husband's well-being. Although he was constantly active—far *too* active, she often thought —he tired easily, and she knew he was not as strong as he appeared. And yet he insisted that he took good care of himself; he ate sparingly and drank hardly at all, rode horseback whenever he could, and enjoyed the company of his family, his guests, and his staff. "But he does too much," Marie Louise complained to Escoffier. "He cannot say no."

When the royal command came again, this time in the formidable person of the Prince himself, Ritz proved that his wife was correct. The proposal was irresistible. "But what will happen to your 'little house'?" wondered Mme Ritz.

It was decided that Ritz and Escoffier would go to

London, establish the new hotel, and spend no more than six months a year there. Escoffier recommended Gimon, *chef de cuisine* at the Russian embassy in Madrid, to take his place at the Ritz. "Which will not be possible," sighed Marie Louise. Olivier Dabascat, from the Bristol in London and Paillard's in Paris, would be maître d'hôtel. In July 1899 César Ritz and Auguste Escoffier presented their new hotel to London.

# 6

★ ★ ★ ★

# THE ROYAL SLICE OF BREAD

*"Where they go we shall follow."*
*Albert Edward, Prince of Wales*

It was at the opening of the Carlton that Auguste Escoffier presented the final version of his peach dessert to Dame Nellie in the form of *pêches Melba.*

Actually, Auguste had been surprised by the general popularity of the dish he had originally named *les pêches au cygne.* Melba herself demanded it often, with or without the embellishment of the ice swan. But so also did diners who had never heard of Helen Mitchell, the singer who rechristened herself for her home town of Melbourne; they would ask for "that dessert with vanilla ice cream and peaches and strawberries."

By 1899, Escoffier, always dissatisfied with the strawberries, had selected an accompaniment he felt more in contrast to the blandness of the peach and the ice cream: a purée of fresh raspberries. Thus, five years after its initial appearance, the *pêches Melba* popular today was offered on the menu of the Carlton Hotel.

In the more than seventy-five years that have followed, variations have of course occurred. One recipe calls for kirsch in the sauce, another for currant jelly. One suggests the substitution of raspberry jam; another would add a sprinkling of shredded almonds.

There is, in the collection of Dr. J. B. Escoffier, the perfected recipe in Auguste's own hand, describing it as "a most easy dessert to prepare." Here he recommends "casting over the peaches a light mist of spun sugar."

In *The Escoffier Cook Book,* the American edition of *Le Guide Culinaire,* the recipe is indeed simplicity itself. It is, in fact, reduced to two sentences: *"Poach* the peaches in vanilla-flavored syrup. Put them in a *timbale* upon a layer of vanilla ice-cream, and coat them with a raspberry *purée."*

Besides Marie Louise's favorite toast, there were other "Melba" creations. *Les ris de veau Melba* were veal sweetbreads in a mustard, butter, and lemon sauce, accompanied by asparagus tips and mushrooms. *Garni Melba* called for small tomatoes stuffed with minced chicken and truffles in a *velouté* sauce, topped with bread crumbs and baked. *Fraises Melba* and *poires Melba* were variations of the peach dessert substituting strawberries and pears.

Other famous singers immortalized on Escoffier menus include Enrico Caruso, with spaghetti in a marinara, mushroom, and chicken-liver sauce; Luisa Tetrazzini, with diced chicken in a rich cream-and-cheese sauce over pasta; and Adelina Patti, with breast of chicken on sautéed *gnocchi,* with truffles and creamed artichokes.

Among the composers were Meyerbeer, with his famous eggs; *filets de sole Verdi,* the fish laid over diced macaroni and lobster, and glazed with *sauce Mornay;* and Rossini, whose name on menus is practically synonymous with a garnish of truffles and foie gras in a Madeira demi-glace.

The new hotel was constructed on the terrace where once the Prince Regent's palace had stood. Although the shell of the building had already been raised when Ritz arrived back in London, he and Mewès went over the plans and, to the distress of the financial backers, made changes.

Typically, Ritz insisted on a garden, and where there was no room for one, he created a Palm Court with moveable panes of frosted glass and tropical plants. One of the workmen remembered that once the Carlton Terrace was *all* garden, and nightingales sang there.

Ritz also wanted a private balcony where the Prince of Wales and his friends could "have their coffee and listen to the orchestra undisturbed."

Still objecting to the cost, one of the directors demanded how often Ritz expected His Royal Highness to dine at the Carlton.

"Very frequently," Ritz replied.

And Harry Higgins, the solicitor who had once said, "Kings and princes will be jealous of you, Ritz; you are going to teach the world how to live," now advised, "Don't stop him. He knows what he's about. Go ahead, Ritz; have your drama."

As it turned out, the Prince of Wales did indeed dine frequently at the Carlton, setting a precedent when he dined there *in public.* Escoffier kept a little book of his favorite menus and dishes.

As for the secluded balcony, Albert Edward simply said, "Do palms grow in your hotels, Ritz? They seem to!"

It begins to grow repetitious to describe the fantastically successful opening of each of Escoffier's and Ritz's hotels. "They moved from triumph to triumph," wrote Marie Louise.

The apparent marvel of the Carlton was that every bedroom had its private bath, a hitherto-unknown luxury and extravagance. Mme Ritz and her sons had come on ahead from Paris, but beyond checking the linens and the crystal-and-silver powder boxes in the cloakroom, "which looked like a great lady's private boudoir," she found little to do. The "Ritz idea" was well known by this time, and the English had taste in flower arrangements. Furniture and decoration were carried out in styles of the eighteenth century.

On opening night the carriages of "all London"

reached from the Haymarket to Piccadilly Circus, and up Pall Mall to Waterloo Place. The Prince of Wales canceled a party at the Savoy in order to be on hand. And all went as serenely and superbly as Escoffier's and Ritz's followers had come to expect.

But the London of 1899 had come a long way from the city of ten years before when D'Oyly Carte had seen his second dream come true.

In those days it was almost unheard of for a family of means to dine out together on a Sunday, or even to wish to. Now Sunday dinner at the Carlton, like *"Les Dimanches"* at the Ritz, became a special occasion. Sometimes as many as five hundred diners were served on those long afternoons after church, while their servants were set free to attend services themselves or to regale their families with the goings-on upstairs. And the English were no longer resigned to what Coquelin called their "cold joint and gloom on Sundays."

It had been Ritz who had urged Parliament to pass laws allowing restaurants to stay open on Sunday, and also until 12:30 A.M. for dinner. Thus Lady de Grey and Harry Higgins, "the heart and soul of Covent Garden," could entertain the operagoers and stars after the performances.

For them, Escoffier created *filets de soles Véronique,* the poached filets glazed with their buttered *fumet* and served around a "pyramid of skinned and very cold Muscatel grapes." Today we are accustomed to seeing

*Véronique* on a menu, but at that time it was a startling combination of textures, flavors, and temperatures.

Ritz was anxious that as many aspiring cooks as possible have the opportunity to train under his colleague; he readily saw the future advantage for them of such an apprenticeship. Sometimes there would be as many as sixty chefs in Escoffier's kitchens. This enabled him for the first time to offer his clients a menu that was totally *à la carte.* And so what seems routine and normal for restaurant diners today was an exciting new concept at the Carlton Hotel at the turn of the century.

By this time, of course, there were other well-known restaurants in London.

One of Albert Edward's favorites was Rule's, a secluded eating place in Maiden Lane established in 1798. The walls were covered with prints and paintings; the draperies were plush; and although there was only one private room, it had a hidden entrance and was readily available to His Royal Highness. Perhaps most enticing were the abundance of fine French wines and an adequate French cuisine. There was also good British fare: grouse, pheasant, Scotch salmon, jugged hare, steak-and-kidney pie, and a rich, redolent trifle.

One went to the Carlton "if one wanted a more lavish meal," as an account of the time explains. The "meal would cost more, but not much more." For less than three pounds, a fortunate couple could dine upon "oysters; soup; filet of sole served in piecrust with vermicelli and crayfish tails, flavoured with champagne and Parmesan; *noisettes de chevreuil Diane* [flamed venison]; *suprêmes de volaille au paprika* [chicken breasts]; then ortolans cooked in earthenware *cocottes* and served with grapes . . . and Benedictine 'roses' [cherries in liqueur]."

All this "while one reclined in large armchairs in the cream-and-pink lounge where pale blue light fell on the palms and the band played a Hungarian *mazurka.*"

It is hardly any wonder that when the time finally arrived, Albert Edward chose the Carlton for his gala coronation banquet.

The Prince of Wales became King of England at 6:30 P.M., January 22, 1901. His mother died, not in his arms, but in those of her grandson, the Kaiser Wilhelm II, whom Bertie disliked and distrusted. He called him "an impetuous and conceited youth," and when he referred to "my illustrious nephew," he did so with a wink. Wilhelm, in turn, called his uncle "a vain old peacock."

The new King, his mother having already decreed that there could be but one Albert, chose the name "which has been borne by six of my ancestors," and set his coronation date for June 26, 1902.

He was nearly sixty, and a grandfather; it was long past time for him to be king. But, since the rule of George III, a year or so of court mourning had been customary. The end of June promised good weather for the festivities, and by that time the unpopular South African war must surely be over. Needless to say, the Carlton was fully booked as soon as the date was made known.

Edward wasted not a moment in designating his friends' hotel as the center for most of the celebrations outside Buckingham Palace. Not only were the most luxurious accommodations available, and the finest cuisine in the world, but the hotel also happened to be situated right on the coronation route. Those who had not booked rooms on Pall Mall would have reserved window seats on that side.

All of this came as a combination of delight and consolation to Ritz and Escoffier. They had always known that as King of England their friend would no longer be at liberty to come and go among them with his set as had long been his custom. Still, they rejoiced in his ascent to the throne for his sake and for the country's. Victorian England had not been a happy place for many years. The Edwardian Era, as it was already beginning to be called, promised a freer and more joyous atmosphere.

As the great day approached, Ritz and Escoffier filled every hour with preparation. In a way, César must have realized that it was for this that he had left his *"petite maison"* in Paris and come to London. Many nights he returned exhausted to his family in Golders

Green. Marie Louise's pleas to him to rest fell on deaf ears. He did not know how to rest. A hotelkeeper must constantly strive to surpass himself, he reminded his anxious wife. He must constantly provide something new, something better, for his guests whom he has educated in luxury. "I know what they want today, but what will they want tomorrow?" he worried.

Furthermore, he had vowed that the hotel the Prince had honored would now honor the King.

Reflecting this pride, Escoffier created new dishes named for the King and Queen: *selle d'agneau de lait Edouard VII, poularde Edouard VII, mousseline de saumon Alexandra, timbale de cailles Alexandra.*

The King himself planned the coronation banquet with Escoffier. Always concerned with pomp and ceremony, he went over and over every detail. Guests from around the world would be in court dress; the decorations, music, wine, and particularly the menu must be worthy of their presence. They had, after all, been waiting for this for a long time.

So had the "people." It had been over sixty years since there had been a coronation; very few of them had ever seen one. More than that, they had also been deprived of the pageantry of a royal wedding. Deep in mourning, Victoria had decreed that her son's marriage be performed quietly at Windsor Castle instead of splendidly at Westminster Abbey. Now subjects from all over the realm came to see the flags and banners going up along the streets, and they decorated their own houses, too.

Then, several days before the ceremony was to take place, the head chef at the French embassy received a telephone call from his friend, the head chef at Buckingham Palace. The King, it appeared, had not been eating well. In fact, he had hardly any appetite at all.

This in itself was so unusual that the head chef at the French embassy called *his* friend, the head chef at the Carlton Hotel, with the news, adding that the King had not even appeared at the state banquet at the palace that evening.

In his reassuring way, Escoffier suggested that it was doubtless a combination of excitement and fatigue affecting His Majesty, and that once the coronation was over, all would be well again. He was busy in his little study off the main kitchen when another call came. "Auguste," César was saying, "come at once."

Escoffier sighed. It was not unusual to be summoned a few days prior to a banquet; this just happened to come at a particularly inconvenient moment; it was nearly noon, the time he normally spent supervising lunch preparations. But his confrère would have known that. And Ritz's tone had been urgent.

Escoffier tapped at Ritz's door, not having the slightest idea whom he might find there. He found no one but César, who announced, "A bomb has fallen. There will be no coronation."

Escoffier thought first of all of what could possibly have happened to the King, then of what would happen to the banquet, and finally, naturally, of all the leftover food.

Ritz was putting on his elegantly tailored frock coat, pinning his white carnation to the silk lapel, and calling his staff together. Quietly he told them that His Royal Highness was undergoing emergency surgery, and that the coronation had been indefinitely postponed. He thanked his staff for the monumental effort they had made in behalf of King Edward VII and the Carlton Hotel, lifted his hand in a gesture of dismissal, and proceeded to the restaurant. Here is an account from *The Times:* "The luncheon room was quite full; we were struck by the animation . . . eager conversations in nearly all languages . . . then suddenly silence. Everyone stood up to see why. In the middle of the room, M. Ritz, pale and dejected, was speaking in a muffled but audible voice: 'The coronation will not take place.' "

At four o'clock that afternoon César Ritz returned to Marie Louise in a state of collapse. His coachman helped him to the door; a doctor had already been summoned. A complete nervous breakdown was diagnosed. In those days that was treated only with rest. For how long must he rest? Mme Ritz wanted to know. "Maybe a few months," she was told, "maybe a year. Maybe longer." Actually, he never did recover.

As for Escoffier, he gathered up the two thousand quail, hundreds of chickens and lambs and hams, fancy ices and decorated cakes, and sent them off to the Little Sisters of the Poor.

And as for the King, when the royal physicians broke the news to him, he declared in typical fashion that he would rather be dead than miss his coronation. He would go if it killed him, he said. Then, more conciliatory: "Obey your consciences and do your duty, if you cannot spare me the pain of inflicting this great disappointment on the civilized world, whose representatives have honoured me with their presence in London."

His condition was described to the stunned public as perityphlitis, an inflammation similar to appendicitis. Upon recovering, his first act was to set a new coronation date.

On that August day, the seven priceless pearls bestowed upon Caterina by her uncle, the Medici Pope, on the occasion of her marriage, were seen for the last time on a royal head. After the ceremony, Edward sent Clement's gift to the Tower along with the rest of the crown jewels.

The next few years were exciting and resplendent ones. Although the new King was not universally popular (Henry James referred to him as "fat, vulgar, dreadful Edward," and others objected to his seeming frivolity: his mistresses, gambling, and other indulgences; his frequent trips to the Continent; an apparently pleasure-seeking existence), the average Briton loved his "good old Teddy."

His father, known to many of them only as "the German," had *not* been universally loved. He was considered stiff and stuffy, and then, of course, he was a foreigner. And "Teddy's" mother sometimes seemed to them to have spent most of her time either in mourning or seclusion or both. So the general attitude of the people was one of thankfulness that their new King had been able to withstand the stultifying influences of Buckingham and Windsor. They rejoiced with him when his horses won at Ascot; they praised his efforts at peace-keeping (most of his Paris jaunts were for that purpose); and they admired England's most beautiful Queen.

Abroad he became increasingly popular. His deep concern about the likelihood of conflict in Europe, and ways to avoid it, touched men of many nations, who, like him, had seen the gathering clouds. During his first state visit to Paris in 1903, after a long absence (the one that had kept him from the opening of the Ritz), the French forgot their differences over the Boer War and cried, *"Vive nôtre Roi!"* Unable to negotiate a peace resolution with the nephew he had never cared for, he turned his back on the Kaiser and his attention to the achievement of an entente cordiale, in which he managed to include Russia after a controversial visit to St. Petersburg in 1908.

The Edwardian Era has been called the "golden summer of the British Empire." Actually, it was more of an Indian summer. But the hosts and hostesses of London, too long subdued by a monarch they hardly knew and seldom saw, burst upon the social scene with an expansiveness and abandon that can best be called an understandable revolt against the restrictions they had suffered through Jubilee after Jubilee of Victorianism.

With Escoffier, now world-famous, at the Carlton, that hotel became the center of this spontaneous expression. Although the King himself did not come to dine, his friends did, and Escoffier found himself engulfed in a frenzy of balls and receptions. That he missed César Ritz goes without saying. He also missed his visits to France. Whereas formerly he had been able to spend part of his time in Paris, now, with Ritz gone, he felt compelled to give their new establishment most of his attention. In spite of his unwillingness to learn English, there were times, he confessed, when he considered London more than any city on earth his true home.

A typical morning would find him rising at six-thirty. In the old days he would have gone to the markets himself: Covent Garden, or, in Paris, Les Halles Centrales. Now he sent trusted envoys; and by seven o'clock, in his Louis Philippe dress coat, he was in the kitchens to inspect what had arrived for the day's tables.

There might be songbirds, foie gras, *pré-salé* lambs, truffles, Normandy butter, and young vegetables and fruits from France; Hamburg beef, Black Forest filets, and sauerkraut from Germany; garbanzo beans, Málaga grapes, and pepper-cured Xerica hams from Spain; and polenta, Bologna sausages, macaroni, and Parmesan cheese from Italy.

In huge wicker baskets labeled RESERVED FOR THE CARLTON HOTEL, LONDON came Malossol caviar, smoked eels, and dried meat from Russia; salt cod, pickled herring, and Edams from Holland; rice, powdered curry, and sago from India; coffee beans from South America; Cape wines from South Africa; pineapples and chocolate from the Indies; and yams, guavas, and sugar from America.

And from all over the British Isles came sole, turbot, salmon, and Colchester or Whitstable oysters; Aylesbury ducklings; game birds in season; Irish and Yorkshire fowls; Scottish beef and red deer; Wiltshire lamb and Southdown mutton; York hams; leafy vegetables; Kent apples; and the cheeses: Stilton, Cheshire, Wensleydale, and Caerphilly.

Ascertaining the quality, freshness, and lasting capacity of these, and also what might be demanded by expected guests, Escoffier drew up the menus for the day. Then he had a breakfast of tea and biscuits brought to him in his office.

Afterward it was back to the kitchens to supervise the preparation of the lunch dishes, and particularly to observe the general atmosphere around him. In a profession known to breed and foster temperament, Escoffier would not allow his chefs to quarrel. "The rush hour is not the signal for a rush of words," he maintained.

There was to be no time for jealousies, vulgarity, profanity, or flares of temper. Smoking and drinking (except for barley water) were forbidden, as were practical jokes. Remembering all too well the restaurants of his youth, where the motto was "If you want to keep your appetite, keep out of the kitchen," Auguste managed both cleanliness and discipline without ever raising his voice.

When he felt he was becoming incensed because of some stupid mistake or misconduct by an apprentice, he would reprimand the culprit gently and then say to himself: I am going out; I can feel myself getting angry. And he would leave the kitchen with a few crumbs in his pocket to feed the pigeons and a few shillings to feed the poor.

He had heard that once Ritz had grabbed a knife from an incompetent carver and threatened him with it. An hour later he was praising the fellow for his **expert** boning of a trout. "If a thing was done well," said Olivier Dabascat, "he was the first to remark it; if badly, he was a veritable lion." But Escoffier had already learned the value of keeping his emotions under control.

By eleven o'clock he would be in the restaurant, checking the reservations with the maître d'hôtel. If the guests included some whose tastes he knew, he would suggest that their headwaiters recommend particular dishes. To be sure of pleasing all his patrons, whether familiar or not, he would inquire about the number in each party, the ratio of men to women, the nationality of the group, and the amount it might wish to spend. Then he would consider with the sommelier what wines should be suggested.

Sometimes he would lunch in the restaurant with a friend, but usually he dined lightly before the service began, and spent the lunch hour in the kitchen, sniffing a sauce, rearranging a garnish, testing the warmth of a platter, and maintaining order with dignity and authority.

In the afternoons he would walk, rapidly and in all kinds of weather, to see his suppliers, or visit a new food shop or market, or discuss with other chefs the whimsical tastes of their clients. "Novelty!" he wrote. "It is the prevailing cry; it is imperiously demanded by everyone."

By six he was back in his kitchens, supervising the preparation of dinners that might run from seven until one. No diner was allowed to feel hurried. All must be permitted to enjoy looking over the menu, consulting the waiters, and dining in a manner as relaxed as in their own homes.

If Escoffier had no invitation to join a group in the restaurant, or had no plans to attend the theater, his chief outside interest, he would dine alone in his office or in his fifth-floor apartment, around nine o'clock, on vegetable soup with rice and fresh fruit. Then he would work on the next day's menus, or on an article for a culinary magazine, or on his own cookbooks, which, remembering the urging of Urbain-Dubois years ago, he was dutifully compiling.

Midnight found him once more in the Carlton's kitchens, where now only about a dozen cooks were on duty. After-theater suppers were more or less the same each night; only rarely were there last-minute demands for special dishes at that time.

What Escoffier was concerned with now was *les restes,* the leftovers. He saw them not so much as remnants of past dishes but as possibilities for the future. What could be transformed into a new dish, or used as part of a soup or sauce, a soufflé or croquette?

Distressed with the extravagances he had seen where he once worked, he had resolved long ago that nothing in *his* kitchens should go to waste. In those days of acknowledged excesses, Escoffier's attitude was considered eccentric, to say the least. Still, in a genius, and especially an untemperamental genius, eccentricity could be forgiven and hostesses merely smiled when they heard of the barquettes, *suprêmes,* and terrines remade, renamed, or enjoyed by the Little Sisters of the Poor.

As at the Ritz, it was the ladies whom the Carlton endeavored most to please. Food, and the delicacy of its presentation, was largely directed toward them; the dining room, with its profusion of flowers and discreet corners, was designed for their entertaining. Whereas during the Victorian Era the grand parties were held behind the closed doors of Mayfair and Belgravia, it was now not only condoned but popular to go where one could see and be seen, and, best of all, dine on the divine offerings of the great Escoffier.

Years before, Lady de Grey and Mrs. Langtry had initiated at the Savoy the custom of holding dinner parties in public. Now Lady Warwick and Mrs. Alice Keppel, both favorites of the King; Lady Randolph Churchill, whose husband, "Gooseberry-face," had helped relax the liquor-licensing laws so that drinks could be enjoyed on Sundays; Consuelo Vanderbilt, the Duchess of Marlborough; and Margot Asquith, lively wife of the Prime Minister, presided at *intime* gatherings of twenty or so.

The gentlemen wore tails and gloves, and carried top hats and canes; the ladies, in decolleté evening dress, coiffed their hair elaborately with feathers and jewels. César Ritz's flattering backgrounds—staircases, mirrors, and indirect, soft lighting—never failed to enhance the scene. And his habit, still carried on, of placing RESERVED cards on the most desirable tables never failed to please the old aristocracy.

Escoffier remembered his confrère when he saw these "Ritz touches," and he often thought of the days when they had been busy and happy together.

In the meantime, the Carlton Company was planning to build a new hotel at Piccadilly and Green Park where the old Walsingham and Bath Hotels had just been torn down. Louis Sherry had tried in vain to buy the valuable land. Now the first steel-framed building in England was going up, and it was to be named for César Ritz.

Mewès, the architect, had consulted Ritz about the plans and decor, suggesting Louis XVI style throughout. César, far from well, had told his friend to do what he wished. "You know by now what my ideas are," he added.

There were some who called it "Mewès's Folly" and wondered why a new luxury hotel was necessary. The company pointed out that great balls were still being held in town houses: Dorchester and Londonderry in Park Lane, Landsdowne in Berkeley Square, Devonshire in Piccadilly. And why? Simply because there were not enough de luxe hotels. Even America, it was reported, surpassed Britain in this respect.

The London Ritz opened in 1905, an all-steel structure costing, rumors said, nine hundred thousand pounds. With its view of the luxuriant park, its gold-leaf-and-crystal chandeliers, its pink marble columns and silver inkstands, its Victorian sculpture and hand-carved paneling, its tapestries, bronze garlands, long mirrors, Persian carpets, Louis XVI furniture, and jardinières of palms, it had "an elegance suited to monarchs and shy millionaires wishing to remain incognito."

Neither in size nor in character did it resemble the Savoy or the Carlton. Although termed "Edwardian baroque," it seemed more like Ritz's "little house" in Paris.

Later, when Harry Higgins, because of the hotel's triumphant success, contemplated enlarging the property, he ran into unexpected difficulties with his new neighbor. No, declared Lord Wimbourne, he would *not* sell his house to provide room for a wing for Higgins's venture. He had, as a matter of fact, been planning to enlarge his garden. How much would Higgins take for the Ritz?

Ritz was able to attend the opening, where his devoted "Mimi" reminded him that he had spent his life "making works of art, bringing beautiful things alive, creating new harmonies." He was still in his middle fifties.

Just as Escoffier had feared, however, César soon suffered another breakdown. "I have had to learn to do nothing," he wrote dejectedly from Lucerne. Particularly, he said, he missed *Réveillon* at the Paris Ritz.

*Souper de Réveillon* is the annual supper celebrated by the French after midnight mass on Christmas Eve. Although the feast is traditional, the fare varies according to place and parish. In some households it is a *répas maigre,* a meatless meal featuring oysters, sea urchins, platters of hot and cold *fruits de mer,* and a ragout of cod or turbot. In more liberal communities there are: *pâté en brioche, canard au sang, gigot d'agneau en croute, salmis* of pheasant, saddle of hare, and *estouffat de Noël* (stewed beef with wine and brandy).

*Boudins,* both the black and the white sausage puddings, are popular; in French Canada these have been translated into *tourtières:* sausage or pork pies, sometimes shaped like turtles. While turkeys are often served at Christmas dinner, one also appears on New Year's Eve, surrounded by twelve roast quail to symbolize the months ahead. Eggs, and other round or oval shapes, are offered to suggest continuity or unbroken good luck.

Among the *treize* (thirteen) *desserts* at the *Souper de Réveillon* there might be glazed chestnuts, or marrons; *crêpes Noël,* pancakes filled with mincemeat, brandy, and orange-flavored liqueur; *galettes de Noël,* deep-fried sugar-and-honey wafers; and without fail, that eagerly awaited confection, *bûche de Noël,* the French version in cake, butter-cream, and jam of the Anglo-Saxon yule log. Molded and roughly frosted with chocolate and pistachio nuts to resemble a section of tree trunk, it is sometimes wreathed with red roses, and sometimes with holly and mistletoe. A sprinkling of powdered sugar suggests snow.

It is no wonder that Ritz missed such celebrations. But when his old friend the Duke of Orleans sent him a brace of pheasant in consolation, Marie Louise wrote cheerfully that they drank a glass of champagne to his health and happiness.

The brief reign of Edward VII was marked by a unique combination of elegance and frivolity, opulence and sport. Flying had come a long way since the days of Santos-Dumont's free sailing balloon, which set him down in trees or on the roof of the Trocadero Hotel, or required in landing the aid of boys with kites.

After his dirigibles, Santos-Dumont built *Le Cigale Enragé, The Infuriated Grasshopper,* a monoplane whose flight won for him the Legion of Honor. This was in 1904; there were many loyal Frenchmen who never accepted the fact that two American brothers had flown a plane the year before.

Hunting continued as popular as always, particularly
now that motorcars as well as railroads made a day's
covert-shooting party possible as far from London as
the woods of Oxford or the marshes of Ely. The development of the mechanics of hunting guns allowed the
hunters to kill thousands of birds at one outing, and
Edward's son George enjoyed it as much as his father.

There was grouse shooting in August whenever the
court was at Balmoral, and at Sandringham were wild-
life preserves where the King maintained a staff of
gamekeepers to supervise the hatching of ten thousand
pheasant eggs and the rearing of the young. Larders
were built to hold seven thousand hung game. It was
nothing to kill two thousand pheasant in a day.

But there is no question that horse racing was the
favorite sporting event of the Edwardians. From the
Royal Enclosure to the paddock, Ascot glittered like a
jewel, with the ladies in their Worth gowns and the
men with top hats and shooting sticks. Edward's first
Derby victory came with Persimmon while he was still
Prince of Wales. It was a close race, which, a critic
reported, "Persimmon won only by putting out his
tongue." In 1900 the Prince won again with Diamond
Jubilee, which also captured the Grand National.

In 1909 his Minoru won the Derby, making the first
triple win for any English monarch. According to accounts, the crowd was quick to rejoice with their
"Teddy Boy."

As for the royal meals, they continued to be gargan-
tuan, whether served aboard the yacht *Victoria and
Albert,* with a crew of three hundred, several French
chefs, thirty waiters in scarlet livery, gold plate, and a
marine band for dinner music; at numerous castles and
country houses; or Buckingham Palace under the experienced eye of Edouard Nignon, borrowed from
Claridge's. Nignon, who had also worked at the Her-
mitage in Russia, was the author of several cookbooks,
one of which was *Plaisirs de la Table.* He invented a
casserole of roast duck and wine described as tasting
more than any other as "a duck is theoretically expected to taste," a dish he dedicated to Verlaine.

To Edward VII, Edouard Nignon offered *omelette
royale,* the original concept of an omelet filled with a
stuffing and also covered with a sauce. His *omelette
Richemonde* contains mushrooms sautéed in port and
wrapped in the egg mixture, and then finished with a
*sauce Mornay* and browned.

With such a chef in his kitchens, it is hardly any
wonder that the King continued to grow immense.
Alexandra, who like John Lyly believed that eating was
good for the brain ("Eat enough and it will make you
wise"), did not deter him. Neither did his lady friends,
who still somehow managed to keep their hourglass
figures. But there were times when Edward's coats no
longer buttoned, and he had been known to fall asleep
at the table.

France continued to delight him. He had "discovered" the resort of Biarritz on the Bay of Biscay, as his mother and the Empress Eugénie and Napoleon III had before him. Victor Hugo had written: "I have but one fear, that it may become fashionable." Nevertheless, it was in Biarritz that Edward established a sort of "Spring Palace" where for three weeks at Easter he would relax with his friends, dine at the Café de Paris, and visit the tables of the Casino Bellevue.

One of his most constant companions on these excursions to the seashore was Mrs. Alice Keppel. Although discreetly accompanied by her two daughters (who were allowed to call Edward "Kingy"), there is no doubt that Alice enjoyed her trips to "wonderland."

On Easter Sunday, for instance, there were Fabergé eggs for all: royal-blue enamel set with a diamond "E" and bearing a tiny gold and ruby crown on top. Then, after church, the party would set out in a motor procession for their annual Easter picnic. The King's automobile with his dog Caesar and Mrs. Keppel led the way; the car with the hampers of food and wine and cigars brought up the rear, well guarded by footmen.

Motoring, as such, was still an unusual undertaking. In his *Motors and Motor-Driving,* Alfred Harmsworth, later Lord Northcliffe, wrote in 1902: "Motoring, for the word will have to be accepted and recognized, is sport." He went on to describe it as a "form of land yachting." No doubt the royal cavalcade, moving along the sandy dunes of the coast, was an engaging spectacle for those living on the route.

To the delight of passing viewers, Edward VII preferred to picnic by the side of the road, possibly because it involved less walking. When he spotted an appealing location, shaded by wind-blown tamarisk trees, he would give the signal to halt, and out would jump the footmen with chairs, tables and tablecloths, silver and crystal. And Mrs. Keppel's little girls would run off to gather wildflowers for "Kingy."

While the crowds gathered to observe this roadside *fête champêtre,* which it pleased Edward to call "impromptu," although he was certainly aware of the effort involved, he would play the game of being incognito. It amused him to adopt an assumed name and talk to the throng as if he were any British tripper on holiday. When Prince of Wales he had sometimes traveled as the "Duke of Chester," or "Baron Renfrew." That his Germanic accent and impressive shape were unmistakable did not seem to bother him at all.

For picnic fare he may have borrowed from Escoffier's recommendations for springtime dining: melon with champagne, a light cream soup, jellied filets of trout, chicken croquettes, pâté of duck, strawberry mousse, and, for the children, *langues-de-chat,* delicate cookies in the shape of a cat's tongue. There might also be local offerings: *poulet Basquais, pipérade, gâteau Basque,* and those old favorites: lobster salad and gingerbread.

All of this was "spiced by iced cup in silver-plated containers. Everything," continues one of the Keppel daughters, "was on a high level of excellence, except the site chosen."

It was after one of these Easter vacations in 1910 that Edward returned to Buckingham Palace more exhausted than refreshed. When urged to taper off his hectic schedule, he protested: "Of what use is it to be alive if one cannot work?"

"And enjoy," he might have added. On the evening of May 4 he wrote sadly in his engagement book: "The King dines alone."

Two days later he was dead.

Marie Louise wrote to Escoffier: "César does not completely comprehend, so it is no longer necessary to shield him from a world grown unreal. But somehow he seems to know that things will not be the same again."

Ritz was right. The Edwardian Era was over, and things would not be the same again. "The face of England has changed overnight," wrote Daisy of Pless.

But it was not the end of the world. The Edwardian Era was, after all, just a "passing day of late summer." And before he knew it, Escoffier was planning the coronation banquet for King George V, to be held at the Carlton Hotel.

The menu that twenty-second of June 1911 included pullet *George V;* baby lamb *de Galles,* for Wales whose prince he had briefly been; the quails he loved to shoot at Sandringham, *aux raisins;* glazed hearts of artichokes *Grand Duc,* a specialty created at the Paris Ritz; and peaches *Reine Marie,* in honor of the new Queen.

That same year the Carlton had a fire. As often happens, it started in a kitchen; a *rôtisseur* allowed a chicken to burn. Calmly Escoffier led his staff to the hotel's roof, whence they were rescued before a tremendous crowd gathered below. With his usual unruffled good humor he remarked, or so it is said, that after all his years of roasting chickens it was only natural one of them should take revenge.

In 1912 Escoffier surprised London by presenting for the visit of King Alfonso XIII of Spain a royal banquet that consisted of a mere seven courses. Furthermore, each course was simplicity itself: melon, consommé, sole *Tosca,* roast saddle of lamb *de Galles,* pullet from Bresse, a Spanish dish of baked eggplant and pimiento with rice, and vanilla ice cream with fresh fruit.

Carême and Soyer would have been dismayed, but it is quite possible that the realistic gourmet Brillat-Savarin would have understood, if not altogether approved.

In any case, Escoffier had seen the health of his friend Edward ruined by gastronomic overindulgences, and he was bound that he would do all he could to prevent this from happening to the present King.

Actually, aside from the game birds he was addicted to, George's favorite food was cream cheese, and whenever he could, Escoffier suggested delicate cream cheese fondants, croquettes, and subtle sauces to please him and guard his well-being.

He also chanced one day in 1912 to please the Kaiser. Urged by the Hamburg-Amerika Line to supervise its kitchens on a few important sailings, Auguste was on board the new 53,000-ton S.S. *Imperator,* afterward rechristened *Berengaria,* when Wilhelm II was to dine. Escoffier presented a whole boned salmon steamed in champagne, and Edward's "impetuous and conceited" nephew was so impressed that he offered the chef anything he desired if only he would come to work for him.

Never at a loss, Escoffier replied that he desired Alsace-Lorraine returned to France, from which it had been snatched during the Franco-Prussian War. Needless to say, he did not go to work for the Kaiser.

A few years later England was at war. At the Carlton, the *sous-chefs* began to complain to their master that, because of war-induced food shortages, *haute cuisine* was no longer possible. And Escoffier, remembering his days on the battlefield of Metz, wrote down from memory the *Menu de Noël* of the Café Voisin in 1870, the ninety-ninth day of the Siege of Paris.

There was the stuffed donkey's head, elephant consommé, loin of camel, tinned "kanguroo," haunch of wolf, and "cat accompanied by rats."

Daubes of young python from le Jardin des Plantes were sometimes available. Genin had served grilled rats as "pigeons," and the Jockey Club had offered rat pie. And for a New Year's party at the Passage des Princes, *both* scalloped elephant trunk and roast bear were served because the host "had connections in high places."

"When a great restaurant must rely on such ingredients for its most festive occasion," Escoffier told his staff, "imagine what the ordinary repasts had to be."

It is hoped that the *sous-chefs* stopped grumbling.

Escoffier stayed on at the Carlton throughout the long years of the war. Late in 1918 came a letter he had been expecting: Ritz had died on October 26 in a private clinic near Lucerne. "A dark cloud seemed to envelop his mind," wrote Marie Louise. "It lifted only at brief intervals during the fifteen years until his death." And then she wrote what others had also said: "He taught the world a new way of living, and a better one than it had known before."

At the end of the letter was a pathetic postscript. Her younger son, René, was also dead.

"Come back to the country where you belong," urged Marie Louise.

And Escoffier made plans to do so.

Before he left London, however, he was designated

a Chevalier in the Legion of Honor and decorated with the Cross by the President of France himself, M. Poincaré. Later, in 1928, in an impressive ceremony at the Palais d'Orsay, President Herriot conferred the order of Officier of the Legion upon "one of the finest ambassadors of French taste and tradition." He was the first chef ever to achieve such a distinction. There were many other decorations as well.

And so, past seventy, and still thinking of himself after all the years in London as more of an Englishman than a Frenchman, Georges Auguste Escoffier returned to the warmth and sunlight of the South of France, his native land.

# 7

★  ★  ★  ★

## A MAN BEYOND PRICE

*"La bonne cuisine est la base du véritable bonheur."*
G. A. Escoffier

His intention had been to retire quietly in Monte Carlo. On the way he stopped in Paris to see Marie Louise. When César's financial backers in London had expressed their objection to the expense of hiring Auguste for the planning and supervising of the Ritz kitchens, César had told them simply: "A good man is beyond price." Now Marie Louise reminded him of this.

She urged him to stay on at the Paris Ritz as an adviser to her son Charles. But after so many years, Escoffier yearned to go home. Assuring his old friend of the lasting success of the Ritz hotels, he bade her farewell and continued on his way.*

*Escoffier enjoyed a long and reasonably satisfactory marriage. Since, however, Mme Escoffier did not figure notably in her husband's career, preferring the climate of the Riviera to that of more northern locales, she is not mentioned elsewhere in this book. Suffice it to say that she undoubtedly influenced his decision

For a while, he was content in his retirement. He continued to write, compiling *Ma Cuisine,* which would be a companion volume to his already famous *Guide Culinaire.* He gardened, and now and then sketched flowers as he had done when a boy, and he chatted with local chefs in their offices and kitchens.

His fame by now was legendary. He had received honors and decorations. His books, articles, and reviews, with their precise and detailed instructions, as well as theories of modern cuisine, were known the world over. He had friends from the royal houses of Europe, in the theater and the opera, in literature and other arts. Visitors soon discovered La Villa Fernand on the avenue de la Costa.

"I have no time for myself," he wrote to Marie Louise. "Formerly I could at least close my office door. Now my garden gate swings all day long."

Through that garden gate one afternoon came a lady in distress. It was the widow of Jean Giroix, the young chef who had worked with Escoffier at the Petit Moulin Rouge, and later had left César Ritz with the advice that he ask Escoffier to take his place. Escoffier had often mused that he and Ritz might never have met had not Jean Giroix been lured to a better-paying position.

---

to retire to Monte Carlo, where she prepared all his meals because, as Escoffier took pride in saying, she was a better cook than he was! He survived her by only a few weeks.

Now Giroix was dead, leaving his wife with two hotels to manage. They were, she confessed, too much for her. Was there any chance that the great Escoffier might be willing to help her with this burden? To her never-ending surprise, Auguste agreed to assist in the administration of the kitchens of the Hôtel de l'Ermitage.

No one knew how much he had missed his old life. Now, working again in Monte Carlo, he was able to make use of the familiar herbs of his native Provence. There was rosemary for *poulet aux olives, canard au vin rouge,* and particularly for *selle d'agneau;* there was thyme for *oeufs à la Bourguignonne, terrine de volaille, boeuf Bordelaise,* and innumerable *cassoulets.* There was fennel for *huîtres à la Florentine,* and *bouillabaisse Marseillaise;* and marjoram for *rôtis d'agneau, gigôt de mouton,* and *oignons à la Monégasque.*

There was also tarragon for the sauces *Béarnaise, Ravigote,* and *Niçoise,* for *mayonnaise vert,* and *poulet sauté à l'estragon;* basil for *soupe au pistou, ratatouille,* and *salade de homard;* savory for *caneton Nantais* and *haricots blancs;* redolent anise for *potages.*

And there was sage for *filet de boeuf en croustade, veau farçi,* and *polenta aux foies de volaille.* (A local saying was: "He who has sage in his garden has no need of doctors.") There was chervil for *omelettes aux fines herbs, champignons à la Grecque,* and *sauce Vincent;* and saffron for *poulet à l'Espagnol,* and rice, tea cakes, and buns.

There were bay leaves for ragouts and the *bouquet garnis* indispensable to French cooking. There was parsley for *escargots, crevettes à la Bordelaise, jambon persillé,* and soups and salads, stuffings and sauces.

Above all there was garlic, that pervasive and persuasive odor of Provence, for sole (and anything) Provençale; for *rouille* for *bouillabaisse; bagna cauda,* the "hot bath" for cold vegetables; *aïoli,* oldest of sauces; and a multitude of Mediterranean repasts.

Much of this was regional food, even peasant fare. It was a far cry from the prescribed elegance and designated restrictions of the *haute cuisine* expected by his clients in London and Paris. There was no doubt of the challenge of presiding over kitchens where such dishes, in addition to the classical, were prepared.

Georges Auguste Escoffier's last years were, like all the others, predominantly happy and successful. Aside from l'Ermitage, he also undertook the supervision of the kitchens of a new hotel, the Riviera.

He traveled to many capital cities to advise chefs, receive honors, and lend a moment of supreme prestige to a restaurant. And, as in the days of "his" Prince of Wales, patrons followed and diners rejoiced. He even crossed the ocean to America, where he enjoyed those delicacies of East Coast cuisine: canvasback, terrapin, and chicken Maryland.

For many years his health and well-being flourished, nurtured by the sun and the salubrious fragrant air of his beloved South of France. The fogs and snows of London were behind him forever, but he never heard the names of Edward and Alexandra, D'Oyly Carte, Nellie Melba, or Sarah Bernhardt without a smile and a token toast in a Côtes de Provence rosé.

On the twelfth of February 1935 Escoffier died in his home, la Villa Fernand. He was eighty-eight. Two weeks before, he had been admitted to a clinic in Nice, the city where he had begun his long and remarkable career. The doctors there diagnosed an incurable case of uremia.

Escoffier told them that he did not wish to end his days in a clinic, as his friend Ritz had. The doctors understood and sent him back to Monte Carlo. He was buried in his family's vault at Villeneuve-Loubet. A year later a marble statue of him was erected in the cemetery.

Today his parents' old stone house is a museum in his honor. There in the kitchen is the huge, deep fireplace with its spit and marmite, iron pots, and wooden spoons and bowls. And outside in the garden the herbs still grow. There are violets in the woods, and in the fields tobacco lifts its green stalks.

How does one determine superiority? How can we assess achievement? Ask someone to name the first color he thinks of: the answer is apt to be red. The first flower is usually the rose; the first bird, the robin. Try it with the first chef, and after a moment's hesitation, perhaps, Escoffier is the one.

But superficial knowledge of a man, and his popularity, are not standards of greatness.

With César, Escoffier ironically and unwittingly gave to the name "Ritz" a connotation of high style, haughtiness, and even snobbery that would have distressed them both. "The Ritz is *not* ritzy," César's son Charles maintained. But even so the myth prevails. It is hopefully emulated. There is an all-night bar and grill in a small town in Nova Scotia called the Ritz. In Dublin there is a "Ritz Restaurant" advertising "Take Away Food," and at the port of the city, a "Ritz Café, Fish and Chips." At a Ritz Hotel in India, the only dessert, Jell-O, is served from a refrigerator in a corner of the dining room.

What hostess has not bought Ritz crackers or Ritz silver-polishing cloths, assuming them to be the very best? There are Ritz beauty salons, Ritz movie theaters, Ritz cleaners, and Ritz dog kennels. A song called "Putting on the Ritz" was popular at about the same time as another called "Stomping at the Savoy." The general use, or misuse, of the word in our language is apparently here to stay.

Webster defines "ritzy" as "ostentatiously smart in appearance or manner." But perhaps it is best summed up in Charles Ritz's account of the American girl in his Paris hotel who looked up at his father's portrait and said: "You mean, there really was a man named Ritz?"

The well-known and elegant Ritz Hotels of Paris, London, Madrid, Lisbon, Montreal, and Boston, among others, attest to the high standards of decorum set so long ago by two men who changed the dining habits of their world.

Almost against his will, Escoffier left us an inheritance of his cookbooks. There never seemed to be time for writing. Future glory meant little to him; there was too much at hand to be accomplished.

Nevertheless, with a consuming desire to share, and urged on by his old adviser, Urbain Dubois, in 1903 Escoffier, with Philéas Gilbert and Emile Fétu, published *Le Guide Culinaire* in Paris. This was translated into English, German, Swedish, and Italian, and in 1941 it was brought out in America as *The Escoffier Cook Book*.

In 1910, with the same collaborators, Auguste published *Le Livre des Menus.* Intended as a companion volume to *Le Guide Culinaire,* it was a collection of menus from the Savoy and Carlton days. Some of them had been offered to the occasional diner, but most had been created for particular and often important patrons to be presented at banquets, formal dinner parties, or intimate suppers. Recognizing their possible value to him in preparing future repasts, Escoffier had preserved his notes and instructions, whether by telephone, letter, or a visit by the client to his office. He maintained that the composing of menus was "among the most difficult problems of our art, and it is in this very matter that perfection is so rarely reached."

A year before his death, *Ma Cuisine, Traité de Cuisine Familiale,* another great compilation of recipes in the manner of *Le Guide Culinaire,* appeared. Escoffier called it a "guide to everyday cooking." In it he recommended that, for one's best health, meat and vegetables be eaten together; that "a good and fine dinner should preferably end with fruit"; that "the new-laid egg, lightly cooked in its shell, is easily digested and nourishing"; that coffee "revives the mind"; and that "it is advisable to leave the table without having satisfied one's appetite to repletion."

And then this reminder: "One must not forget that good sound cooking, even the very simplest, makes a contented home." The chef to emperors and admirals never forgot the humble hearth.

The column in *L'Art Culinaire,* which Auguste began in 1894 and called *"L'Ecole des Menus,"* was a guide to planning meals in the modern home, hotel, and restaurant. There were also reviews from time to time in the *Chronique de Londres* and *Carnet d'Epicure.* Well aware of the contributions of his predecessors and colleagues, Escoffier acknowledged them with respect.

He even found time to set down reminiscences of

his war days: *Memoires d'un Soldat de l'Armée du Rhin. Les Fleurs en Cire,* published in 1885, contained instructions for the making of wax flowers, an art he had learned in Nice when stationed in an army camp there. The book also contained ideas for table decoration, and even a bit of verse; he wrote not only with correctness but also with charm.

For Prosper Montagné's *Larousse Gastronomique,* that revolutionary chef's immense compilation of "food, wine, and cookery," Escoffier supplied a generous and appreciative preface. "While waiting to read them in print," he wrote, "I went through the innumerable manuscript pages of this encyclopedia and I am still under the spell cast by this work."

He was not able to wait "to read them in print," but his friend Philéas Gilbert wrote a second and confirming preface to the huge work whose first edition, with its eighty-five hundred recipes and descriptions, finally saw the light of day in 1938. "Like Escoffier, I wish heartily that such a magnificent and persevering effort may find its reward . . ."

Montagné wrote other books, including *Les Delices de la Table,* and presided over a restaurant in the rue de l'Echelle generally considered one of the best in France. On the centenary of Brillat-Savarin's death, Montagné planned a dinner party at the Crillon, although it was Carême he most admired. He found his notes in Talleyrand's archives!

As for Escoffier's most famous creations, there are many opinions. Perhaps *pêches Melba* and Melba toast come most readily to mind. But there were also *poularde Derby;* probably *tournedos Rossini,* named for the composer who "retired early to devote the rest of my life to gastronomy" and strewed his repasts with foie gras and truffles; *bombe Nero; cuisses de nymphes à l'aurore;* and a *soufflé au Parmesan* (using ten eggs and baked in a silver mold) that he made popular in London.

It is interesting that Eugéne Herbodeau and Paul Thalamas, who wrote invaluable memoirs of their master, include as his best-known dishes: *médaillon de volaille à l'Isabelle, célestine de homard à la Mogador, chaud-froid de mauviettes* (larks) *en cerises,* and *aspic de langouste à la Cléopatra.*

They also mention a *salade japonaise aux fruits,* created for a dinner at the Carlton given by the Japanese embassy for visiting Japanese bankers. Cubes of pineapple, orange sections, and whole cherry tomatoes were served on lettuce with a dressing of fresh cream, salt, and lemon juice. "Escoffier sometimes hazarded very bold culinary inventions which produced the most delicate results. It is the mark of a true artist," his friends conclude.

In a brief sketch in *Chambers's Biographical Dictionary,* Escoffier is mentioned as being the inventor simply of the *bombe Nero.*

A bombe, in general, is a frozen dessert, usually of

two ice creams, or an ice cream and a water ice, one encompassing the other, and chilled in a round, oval, or melon-shaped mold.

*Bombe Nero,* as described by its creator, is a center of vanilla mousse, studded with truffle-like bits of chocolate, and coated with vanilla ice cream. Auguste was ever a lover of vanilla. The bombe was then frozen in its mold, unmolded, coated and decorated with meringue, and glazed quickly in a hot oven. Upon serving, it was flamed with rum, producing the "Nero" effect of burning.

Escoffier also offered variations of the *omelette surprise,* made popular by Jean Giroix years before at the Hôtel de Paris. Actually invented by a doctor from Massachusetts practicing in England, it was much like Baked Alaska, a mound of frozen ice cream, often mixed with fruit, piled on a base of *génoise,* or sponge cake, and enveloped in a meringue which is then baked quickly in a hot oven so that the top is browned while the ice cream remains unmelted. In classic cuisine this dessert is called *omelette Norvégienne,* probably for the snow-clad mountain peaks of Norway.

Escoffier had offered variations of it, using bananas and oranges: the fruit was removed from its skins, which were then filled with an appropriate water ice, coated with meringue, decorated, and set on trays of cracked ice to be baked until golden. He had also suggested an *omelette surprise,* flamed and surrounded with cherries in kirsch, reminiscent of *cerises Jubilée,* created in honor of Queen Victoria.

Remembering his mother's kitchen in Villeneuve-Loubet, where fresh milk and cream, potatoes, and Comté, or French Gruyère, cheeses were staples, he had instructed his chefs in the preparation of *gratin de pommes de terre à la Dauphinoise,* recapturing that favorite of his childhood from the Dauphiné: sliced potatoes in milk and butter, baked in an earthenware casserole rubbed with garlic, and laced with *Gruyère française* from the Franche-Comté and the Haute Savoie.

For his old patron, Richard D'Oyly Carte, he had many times produced a variation of this dish: *pommes de terre à la Savoyarde,* substituting consommé for the milk. *Omelette à la Savoyarde* was a pancake-type omelet with fried potatoes and shredded *Gruyère française.* And *Savoyarde,* of course, indicated that mountainous province on the Swiss and Italian borders famous for fine cheeses.

*Pommes de terre Suzette* was another favorite. The potatoes were peeled into the shape of eggs, baked, and then cut lengthwise like a hard-boiled egg. The insides were then scooped out, mashed with butter, cream, chopped breast of chicken, tongue, truffles, and mushrooms, and refilled. The shells, pressed together, were warmed and glazed with melted butter till they looked like brown eggs.

It is impossible to contemplate Suzette without

thinking of crêpes. There are almost as many accounts of the origin of *crêpes Suzette* as there are variations of the recipe. Every chef seems to have his own. The variety lies mainly in the liqueurs used. Grand Marnier, Curaçao, cognac, Cointreau, brandy, and armagnac are variously called for. Escoffier mentions Benedictine and vanilla sugar. And Henri Charpentier, who claims to have invented the dish at the age of fifteen, lists orange-blossom water, kirsch, white Curaçao, maraschino, and rum!

As for the oranges involved, some cooks specify "bright-skinned," some navels, some mandarins, some even tangerines.

Who was Suzette? Charpentier writes that she was the young daughter of a friend of the Prince of Wales who dined with him and her father in 1895 at the Café de Paris in Monte Carlo. When the dessert pancake sauce that the assistant waiter was heating at their table accidentally caught fire, the terrified boy hurled into the pan more liqueur, and served the pancakes anyway, still partially burning.

The Prince, amused as usual, demanded to know the name of this new sweet. At which point, the daughter, Suzette, sprang to her feet and curtseyed, and the Prince bestowed her name upon the dish. "He was," concluded Henri, "the world's most perfect gentleman."

There are, of course, many loopholes in this charming tale. It is highly unlikely that an inexperienced although confident young man of fifteen would be waiting upon the Prince of Wales, let alone entrusted to prepare the royal dessert. And it is just as unlikely that an accidental fire at the serving cart would have gone unnoticed by other diners, waiters, and the maître d'hôtel.

A more plausible explanation for the name is given by André Simon. An actress at the Comédie Française in 1897 was playing the role of Suzette, a maid. At one point she was called upon to serve pancakes. These were provided by the nearby Restaurant Marivaux, and, to attract the attention of the audience, as well as to keep them hot for the actors who had to eat them, they were set aflame. Later M. Joseph, proprietor of the Marivaux, moved on to the Savoy and served his famous dessert to diners there.

Still, it is pleasant to imagine the gallant Prince, the enchanted young girl, and the resourceful boy on the terrace of the Café de Paris while one is enjoying this popular tourists' treat.

"I am quite sure *crêpes Suzette* would not be so much esteemed if they were not served with so much ceremony," observed Mme Ritz, to whom Escoffier offered, besides the toast, those dishes designated *"à la Strasbourgeoise"* and *"à l'Alsacienne."*

It was well known that Escoffier liked to name dishes for occasions: *poularde Derby, cerises Jubilée,* and *suprême de volaille Jeannette.* The chicken breast in aspic with foie gras was named not for a beautiful woman but to commemorate the ship *Jeannette,* which was trapped in Arctic ice floes on an expedition to the North Pole. The shimmering aspic was intended to suggest frozen waters, and sometimes the platter itself was chilled until frosted. André Simon has described *suprême de volaille Jeannette* as "the most popular recipe of the Cuisine Classique for serving cold chicken."

And to commemorate an eruption of Mt. Vesuvius, Escoffier created his *omelette surprise à la Napolitaine,* also called *bombe Vesuve,* which featured a barquette of meringue set in a "Bay of Naples" of glacé chestnut atop a water-ice-coated cake. The whole was quickly browned in the manner of other *surprises* and then set aflame with *cerises Jubilée.*

Finally, there were the celebrated sauces, those "close-fitting" accompaniments to meats and vegetables. "Be painstaking with your sauce," Escoffier wrote. *Sauce Robert* (the word is believed by some to have come from "roebuck" since the sauce originally enhanced venison, although there was also a famous chef, Robert, who taught Carême) and *sauce Diable,* are sometimes simply called "Escoffier" sauces. Boito once told Verdi: "You have the secret of the right note at the right moment." This could be said of Escoffier's creations as well.

But his most important contribution was neither a

famous dish nor a famous cookbook. It was his motto:
*"Faites Simple."*

In spite of such occasional extravagances as "baby's
dream strawberries," culinary art had come a long way
since the days of the "pyramids," *pièces montées,* disguis-
ing sauces, ketchups, and edible or semi-edible,
sculpted concoctions. And the man who shortened
courses and lengthened lives was the one who is still
called "king of chefs, and chef of kings."

The health and well-being, the *bonheur,* of his clients, was constantly uppermost in his mind. No matter
how splendid the appearance, he would not allow his
dishes to be garnished with any material that might be
indigestible; no matter how impressive the presentation, he would not permit his chefs to overload a plate
or platter with a superabundance that could cause
drowsiness or dullness. Indeed, his preoccupations, according to his colleagues, were rapidity of service, the
correct temperature for each dish, and the balance and
easily digestible qualities of the menu.

In a way, he expressed his *philosophie de cuisine* when
he wrote in *Le Guide Culinaire:* "The number of dishes
set before the diners being considerably reduced, and
the dishes themselves having been deprived of all the
advantages which their sumptuous decorations formerly lent them, they must recover, by means of perfection and delicacy, sufficient in the way of quality to
compensate for their diminished bulk and reduced

splendour. They must be faultless in regard to quality; they must be savoury and light. The choice of the raw material, therefore, is a matter demanding vast experience on the part of the chef; for the old French adage which says that *'le sauce fait passer le poisson,'* has long since ceased to be true."

"I love Escoffier," said Lord Northcliffe. "He is a fine chef, and such a restful man." In him were none of the vanity and arrogance of Soyer, the flamboyance of Carême, the temperament and dark despair of Vatel, the trickery of Brillat-Savarin, or the pompousness, vulgarity, and jealousies of lesser artists. His directness and honesty shine through every dish, as they did through his life. Although his mind was constantly at work pleasing the wealthy, his heart was with those less fortunate. "I have been too close a spectator of the sufferings of the poor," he said.

In his introduction to *Ma Cuisine,* André Simon described Escoffier as "always plainly, simply, naturally himself." He came from that part of France where the lightness of nearby Italy tends to influence the native French disposition. Actually, a French chef had never before been more appreciative of Italian cuisine or Italian patrons.

It is hard to think of him without recalling his courtliness, as well as his tact and imagination. Once, when Mme Duchêne, wife of the manager of the London

Ritz, begged him to reveal the true secret of his art, he replied: "Madame, my success comes from the fact that my best dishes were created for ladies."

*"Toute sa vie fut consacrée aux arts utiles"* reads the epitaph of the restaurateur Véry. Are such efforts really worthwhile to achieve so transient a work of art as a dinner? Escoffier was often asked this question. His life reflects his answer.

# TREATS AND RECEIPTS
## *"A Noble Science"*

Robert Burton wrote in *The Anatomy of Melancholy:* "A cook of old was a base knave (as Livy complains) but now a great man in request; cookery is become an art, a noble science; cooks are gentlemen."

From these gentlemen, and a few ladies, we have been left a legacy of descriptions and directions. The following ones seemed to be the most interesting and pertinent. Dishes already described in some detail in previous chapters are naturally not included here.

Some of our earliest written-down recipes come from the fourteenth-century chef to Philippe VI of Valois, Duke of Normandy, and King Charles V. His name was Guillaume Tirel, but he adopted the name of Taillevent, and compiled a cookbook called *Le Viandier.*

Here is what he suggested for the royal duck in those days: "First take some bread and grill it well. Put it to soak in some red wine. Fry some onions in lard. Sift the bread and add some spices —cinnamon, nutmeg, cloves, sugar and salt. Boil all these ingredients together with the fat from the duck which has been previously roasted and pour this sauce over the duck." It was called *caneton à la dodine rouge.*

Another cookbook of the time, *Ménagier de Paris,* written at the request of Charles VI and Isabella of Bavaria, contains an irresistible recipe for *confitures de noix.* "Before St. John's eve gather some fresh nuts. Peel them and make a hole in the middle. Let them soak for nine days, changing the water every day. Dry them thoroughly. Place a clove and a piece of ginger in each hole, put in a pot and cover with honey. The honey must cover the nuts entirely. Three months later it will be ready to eat."

## CHAPTER 1

*Paon en plumage* is a presentation that Charlemagne may have enjoyed, since it achieved royal approval in A.D. 800. It is on record that knights made their vows to it.

The peacock was carefully skinned, stuffed with herbs and spices, and roasted on a spit with its head protected in wet linen. Then it was dressed again in its splendid feathers, tail and aigrettes spread wide, bill and feet gilded.

A wreath of flowers surrounded it, and the mistress of the house would fill the beak with cotton dipped in camphor. When she set the cotton alight, "the bird arrives on the table spitting flames." Incidentally, in gastronomic circles, one does not "carve" a peacock, one "disfigures" him.

*Fagioli all'uccelletto* means beans "like little birds," because their seasoning of crumbled sage, garlic, and peeled chopped tomatoes was intended to give them the flavor of small game.

White beans are used for this dish; if dried they should be soaked overnight. Then they are simmered slowly until just tender in olive oil, water with the appropriate seasonings, salt, pepper, and a splash of wine vinegar as the sauce thickens.

*Tortini de carciofi alla toscana,* the Tuscan artichoke omelet that Catherine de Médicis brought with her from Florence, is made by deep-frying young quartered artichokes and arranging them in a round buttered baking dish; then pouring beaten eggs on top. This is baked briefly in a hot oven until the eggs are firm but still moist, and then browned under the broiler.

Catherine was also fond of artichoke fritters, and there is a recipe for *carciofi Catherine de Médicis* that describes artichoke hearts filled with ground raw pigeon breasts, powdered ginger, cloves, and nutmeg; coated with heavy cream and glazed in a hot oven. Like *fagioli,* artichokes were believed to induce romance.

*Pintade à la Médicis* is a guinea hen stuffed with foie gras, chopped chestnuts, and truffles, and simmered in a covered casserole with a carrot, some minced onion, a pinch of thyme, salt and pepper, a bowl of "good broth," and three glasses of white wine.

Ten minutes before serving time, several larks, stuffed with foie gras and truffles, and lightly browned, are added!

*Carpe à la royale,* as the dish was called when Catherine introduced it to France, was that long-lived member of the goldfish family larded with truffles, placed on a bed of diced vegetables, seasoned "wisely," and drenched with red wine from the Chianti region. It was then cooked very slowly with a few quenelles.

Later it became *carpe à la Maison de France,* and was often served to and by royalty. This revised and elaborated version was poached in domestic Bordeaux, and garnished with sweetbreads, cockscombs, and carp roe.

*Fagioli nel fiasco* is an ancient offering from Tuscany that is said to be Marie de Médici's contribution to French cookery. This time the white beans are simmered in a lightly straw-corked wine flask with a broth of olive oil, water, sage, and garlic, over a charcoal fire.

When done, they are served either hot or cold, with a dressing of oil, salt and pepper, and a little of the bean juice.

*Poule-au-pot,* King Henry IV's desire for each of his subjects'

Sunday dinner, began with placing in an earthenware marmite the stock, vegetables, and herbs that normally went into a *pot au feu,* that nourishing everyday soup.

Then a plump chicken would be stuffed with its heart, liver, toasted bread, a bit of chopped Bayonne ham, sautéed onion, parsley, tarragon, and garlic, bound with eggs, and seasoned with spices.

When the stock boiled, in would go the hen to poach over a slow fire. If there was extra stuffing, it could be wrapped in cabbage leaves and simmered alongside the bird.

Sometimes the strained broth would be served first, as a soup, and then the chicken and vegetables with a gravy of the stock thickened with egg yolks and cream. There are, naturally, many versions of this. One calls for a slice of ham to be added toward the end. Another adds cream, white wine, veal feet, and "good sausage."

Henry himself was not quite so simple in his tastes. Although it has been suggested that "he would eat anything," the traditional *Henri IV* garnish consists of artichoke bottoms with browned potato balls "no larger than hazelnuts," truffles, a rich meat glaze, and *sauce Béarnaise* in honor of the royal birthplace. *Oeufs Henri IV* are, not surprisingly, topped with *duxelles.*

*Perdrix à La Varenne* is an offering from the chef who learned to cook in King Henry's household. The partridges were larded with bacon, browned in butter, and simmered in a lightly seasoned broth. Then they were garnished with truffles, mushrooms, and fricasséed asparagus, and served with lemon and pistachio nuts.

*Sauce Béchamel,* as described by Escoffier, is a white roux thinned with hot milk and combined with sautéed lean veal and an onion, seasoned with salt, mignonette pepper, grated nutmeg, and a sprig of thyme.

The sauce is simmered for an hour, and then strained through a fine sieve. In Lent, "the veal must be omitted."

## CHAPTER 2

The name of Charles Maurice de Talleyrand-Périgord is bound to be associated with the truffles of that region. *Filet de boeuf Talleyrand* is a beef filet studded with truffles, marinated in Madeira, braised with the marinade, and glazed. This is served with a garnish of macaroni, butter, truffles, foie gras, and grated Gruyère and Parmesan. A *sauce Périgueux* with a fine julienne of truffles accompanies the dish.

*Suprêmes de volaille Talleyrand* are chicken breasts cut in heart shapes, poached, and placed on a bed of macaroni (again!) with cream, foie gras, and truffles in a croustade.

On the subject of chicken breasts, *suprêmes de volaille Carême* are stuffed with a julienne of cockscombs and truffles in a mushroom purée, sautéed, set on croutons of fried bread, and garnished with truffles "cut into the shapes of olives and mushrooms." The sauce for this is a veal glaze with tomatoes.

*Laguipière,* the sauce which Carême named for his mentor, is made by adding to 1/4 cup of butter sauce a tablespoon of consommé or chicken or fish glaze, depending on the dish involved, a pinch of salt, nutmeg, vinegar or lemon juice, and "a good piece of fine butter."

For his famous *croquettes de marrons,* Carême prepared a purée of mashed roasted chestnuts with melted butter, cream, eggs, and seasonings. When the purée was cool, he wrapped it around a whole cooked chestnut, rolled it into a ball shape between his palms, and dipped it in beaten egg and then fine bread crumbs.

These croquettes may either be deep-fried or baked in the oven. They are served as an accompaniment to poultry or game.

*Bécasse Carême* is a dish of woodcock, considered by some to be the finest of winged game. Roasted underdone, or "bloody," the breast is cut into four pieces and rolled in mustard and hot lemon juice. Cutting a woodcock is called "thighing."

The remainder of the bird, with its intestines, is chopped, sprinkled with "burnt" brandy, cooked with stock until reduced, and then strained over the breast sections upon which the woodcock's head has been set.

"Everything in a woodcock is good," declared Alexandre Dumas, who then designated it "the queen of the marshes!"

For Brillat-Savarin, the woodcock was in its fullest glory when prepared before the eyes of the hunter who shot it. He ordered the bird to be thighed, browned briskly in butter, simmered, and sauced with the chopped intestines, cayenne, lemon juice, a rich demi-glace, and a wine glass of Madeira.

The pieces are then arranged in a baked pastry shell, garnished with a ragout of cockscombs, kidneys, lamb's sweetbreads, truffles, and mushrooms, and the strained gravy from the wood-cock poured over all.

Then there is the celebrated "Welsh Rare-bit" or fondue that Brillat-Savarin describes as being so creamy that the Bishop of Belley made culinary history by eating it with a spoon.

According to the number of guests, take eggs, and cheese weighing 1/3 of the eggs' weight, and butter weighing 1/6. Beat the eggs, grate the cheese, melt the butter, and place them all in a saucepan on a "good fire," stirring until thick and soft.

"A little salt and a large portion of pepper is added," and it is served up at once on a hot dish. "Bring out the best wine, and let it go round freely, and wonders will be done."

Sally Lunn, that Bath tea cake of the late eighteenth century, has had many tales told of it. Some say it was named for the young girl from Somerset who "cried" the cakes in a basket covered with white linen. Others maintain that because the cakes were round, golden on top, and pale beneath, what she was really crying was "sun and moon," which the French were quick to transpose to *"sol et lune."*

In any case, Bath was a fashionable resort favored by the Prince

Regent, and there is still another story that Carême, visiting there
with the royal entourage, discovered the delicate cake and presented it to his own country "rigged out in the height of French
fashion." And then there was a cake from Alsace-Lorraine called
*"solimême!"*

Most cookbooks include recipes for Sally Lunn, but perhaps not
the words of this ditty written by the Bath baker and would-be
musician W. Dalmer.

> Buy my nice Sally Lunn,
> The very best of Bunn,
> I think her the sweetest of any.

The story of *poulet Marengo* is that it was invented on the battlefield by Napoleon's chef, not Laguipière, but Dunan the Swiss.
The year was 1800; it was a warm evening in June, and, after a
day of fighting, the Bonaparte was hungry. But the Austrians had
ransacked the larder, a supply wagon was lost, the cupboard was
nearly bare.

Dunan dispatched his cooks to the nearby Italian village of
Marengo. They found a chicken, a few crayfish, some eggs,
tomatoes, mushrooms, and garlic; however, there was no butter,
since the villagers cooked only with olive oil. The chef had little
choice but to follow suit.

To make it more palatable, and doubtless to extend it, he
surrounded the sautéed chicken with eggs fried in the same oil,
laid the crayfish across the top, and added a dash of Napoleon's
brandy to the sauce. To his great surprise, Bonaparte was delighted, christened it for the scene of his recent victory, and
demanded it served again and again for good luck.

Alexis Soyer's version: "Fowl, Sauté Marengo, Parisian," in his
*Modern Housewife,* published in 1851, suggests characteristically:
"Take out the fowl, which pile upon your dish, laying the worst
pieces at the bottom."

The now-historic recipe calls for crayfish to be served with the chicken, as in *poulet aux écrevisses.* Since this seemed hardly an appropriate garnish, Dunan omitted them the second time, but Bonaparte, always superstitious about his luck, demanded that the crayfish be restored. According to the *Larousse,* this has become the traditional way of serving the dish. Escoffier agrees.

There is, alas, another story of the famous dish which asserts that it was created in a Paris restaurant to honor the generals returning from Italy. Or might that have been the one made of veal!

The author of *The Three Musketeers* wrote that he intended his last work to be a cookbook "composed of memories and desires." It was. Named for his characters were: *écrevisses à la D'Artagnan,* where the crayfish were simmered with shallots and parsley, and served with a sauce of their stock, egg yolks, butter, and lemon juice; and *homard à la Portos,* in which the lobster was cut up and cooked with butter, vegetables, spices including red pepper, and a bottle of champagne.

He also liked his oysters baked in champagne and glazed with Parmesan.

His "Larks in a Casserole" called for the larks to be stuffed with their "innards," along with chicken or goose livers and truffles. Additional stuffing was placed in the bottom of the baking dish and the birds buried in it so that only their heads poked up. They were then covered with bacon and cooked.

"Just before serving . . . sprinkle the dish with fresh bread crumbs, and rest easy over the results."

And here is Louis XVIII's *l'ortolan restauration,* which he took pride in preparing himself. "You take a dainty little ortolan [a small garden bunting, fattened in cages and served as a delicacy in France], and cook it in the stomach of a partridge which has been lined with foie gras and black truffles."

Francois Tanty, chef to Napoleon III and the Imperial Family of Russia, has left us what must be the simplest rule on earth for charlotte russe. One pound of ladyfingers line a mold; one pound of thick cream is whipped with 1/4 pound of sugar and poured into the mold. "Let cool a little while and knock out."

His _charlotte de pommes_ is "knocked out" and served with an apricot sauce.

## CHAPTER 3

_Aïoli_, the breath and butter of Provence _("l'ail permet tout")_, is a mayonnaise-like sauce made with crushed garlic cloves, egg yolks, a pinch of salt, a fruity olive oil added drop by drop, and a squeeze of lemon juice. It is mixed in a mortar until it is so thick that the pestle stands straight up in it, as Venus, they say, prepared hers!

In a traditional Provençal household, _aïoli_ (which in the old language translated into "garlic oil") is made each Friday, and served on fish, usually salt cod, hard-cooked eggs, artichokes, and boiled potatoes. Upon special occasions, such as a _grand aïoli_ on Ash Wednesday, snails, winkles, and baby octopi appear. Sometimes there will be a _baudroie_, that Mediterranean fish also known as "sea devil." _Aïoli_ seems to come into its own particularly when added to a _bourride_.

_Bourride_ is one of those seafood stews for which, like the more complex _bouillabaisse_ of Marseille, every fisherman and restaurant has a different recipe. The principal fish used are the firm white-fleshed ones: _loup de mer_, sea perch, turbot, cod, John Dory, sole, whiting, brill, even the gray mullet. A single variety, or a combination, is simmered in a court bouillon containing fish stock, leeks, saffron, bay leaves, fennel, diced lemon or orange peel, and dry white wine.

When the fish are tender, the stock is reduced, strained, and with extra egg yolks added to *aïoli,* the *aïoli* is stirred in and beaten till the broth is smooth as cream. In each serving plate is laid a slice of French bread, fried in olive oil and moistened with the stock. Fish filets are placed on top, and the soup is poured around. Sometimes new potatoes come along, with a sprinkle of parsley, and more *aïoli* is passed in a sauceboat.

One cannot leave the soups of the region without a mention of *la soupe au pistou,* that vegetable mélange with the Italian influence.

*Pesto,* called *pistou* or *pestou* in France, is, as its name suggests, blended with a pestle. It is a fragrant mixture of garlic, fresh basil leaves, olive oil, grated Parmesan or Romano, and pine nuts. Created by the voyaging Genoese, it is natural that it should have found its way to the neighboring Niçois country.

Incidentally, the Ligurians maintain that an honest *pesto* can be achieved only from basil growing in their native soil. Sea captains from Genoa carry it with them in pots and urns.

The vegetables in the Provençal soup usually include onions, cut-up potatoes, peeled tomatoes, diced carrots, chopped leeks and celery leaves, white beans, sliced unpeeled zucchini, several saffron threads, herbs and a good deal of pepper, and a little broken pasta "thrown in" near the end.

Off the fire, the *pistou* or *pesto* is blended into the soup (or vice versa), and the whole served with fried bread, chopped parsley, and grated Comté or Parmesan, offered separately.

Toulouse-Lautrec, always an authority on the subject of food, ordered his *soupe au pistou* prepared from "one good plant of basil," and 1/4 pound Gruyère or "Holland cheese."

*Salade Niçoise* is another "moveable feast" as far as ingredients and times and places of serving go. The *Larousse Gastronomique* describes it as a mixture of cooked and cold French beans and potatoes; dressed with oil and vinegar, salt and pepper; decorated with anchovies, black olives, and capers; garnished with quarters of tomatoes; and sprinkled with chervil and tarragon. Not a word about tuna fish.

Why not? It certainly seems to appear in most of the *Niçoise* salads we enjoy today. One thought is that originally it could not be obtained, or afforded.

In any case, this *salade* is traditionally served before the meal, the Italian *antipasto* influence, or even *as* the meal, decoratively arranged on a flat serving platter. Its contents depend somewhat on what is available: in addition to the designated ingredients, quartered hard-cooked eggs, sliced red and green peppers, marinated beets, artichoke hearts, and sprigs of parsley.

The dressing should be of olive oil, wine vinegar, salt and pepper, a bit of mustard, chopped chives and basil, and a scattering of *fines herbes.* It makes a lovely "wherever and whenever" picnic dish.

There is a story that *chaud-froid,* the *velouté* sauce set with aspic, was the result of one of those culinary accidents that sometimes turn into triumphs. In 1759, the Maréchal de Luxembourg was entertaining at a dinner party in his château when he was suddenly summoned to the King's Council. Returning very late, he found that all that remained of his banquet was some fricassée of chicken, cold now, and jelled in its pale rich sauce.

The hungry Maréchal was satisfied, and christened the dish *chaud-froid* (hot-cold) *de volaille.*

Carême began his recipe for *chaud-froid de poulet à la gelée:* "After having lightly singed 5 fine farmyard chickens . . ." and went on to describe its garniture of truffles cooked in champagne, "a very white double coxcomb on top, and a fine border of aspic in two colours cut in decorative shapes."

Escoffier's directions are naturally much simpler. One pint of *velouté* is blended with 3/4 pint of melted poultry aspic, heated, stirred into 1/2 pint of cream, and cooled. At the Savoy he inaugurated the procedure of serving the dish encased in a block of ice.

And Toulouse-Lautrec put it this way: "Lay the pieces [for *poulet en fricassée froid*] in a terrine or deep dish, pour over the gravy, chill, and let jell. Serve cold at a hunting meal in the open air."

*Polpettes de lapereaux rotis à l'Italienne* is an offering of Francatelli, chef and maître d'hôtel of Queen Victoria. A pupil of Carême, he "ventured to offer a few suggestions for the consideration of Epicures."

For his *polpettes,* he combined the chopped meat of two roast rabbits with minced mushrooms, parsley and shallots, grated Parmesan and nutmeg, *velouté* and egg yolks. Spreading this mixture onto an earthenware platter, he stamped it into small rounds, dipped them in crumbs, and fried them "to a light colour over a brisk fire." When done, he would "drain them upon a napkin, dish them up in double circular rows," and serve with brown Italian sauce poured underneath.

For the same Queen, a much younger chef devised dishes to enhance her trips to the Riviera. Garniture Victoria still usually denotes small perfect tomatoes filled with mushroom purée and artichoke hearts in butter with a Madeira sauce.

There followed, from Escoffier: *oeufs pochés Victoria,* the eggs in baked tart shells on diced lobster and truffles, coated and glazed with a lobster-butter sauce; *filets de sole Victoria,* poached sole with lobster, truffles, and crayfish butter in Béchamel sauce; *homard Victoria,* the favorite lobster cut up and served with truffles in a rich white sauce with Madeira and butter; *poularde Victoria,* a chicken stuffed with foie gras and truffles, roasted, and surrounded with diced potatoes in meat jelly; *noisettes de ris de veau Victoria,* sautéed sweetbreads and veal topped with a mushroom-truffle purée, sprinkled with grated cheese, and browned; *tournedos Victoria,* the beef filets sautéed in butter, arranged in a circle with flat chicken croquettes beneath and grilled tomato halves on top; *salade Victoria,* diced lobster meat, truffles, cucumbers, and rice, with a mayonnaise-type dressing seasoned with the lobster coral (if any) or curry; and *bombe Victoria,* a mold coated with strawberry ice, and filled with layers of vanilla ice cream mixed with candied fruit in kirsch, and apricot jam.

One has to be fairly careful about what one names for a queen. I could not find ox tongue Victoria, leg of mutton Victoria, or turnips Victoria.

For her daughter-in-law, the Princess of Wales, Escoffier improvised as many concoctions. Delicate mousselines, sauced, and served with asparagus tips, delighted her. So did *soufflé de jambon Alexandra,* a mixture of minced ham, truffles, Parmesan, and Béchamel, alternated with layers of buttered asparagus tips, and baked till light and fluffy. The surface, mounded like a dome, supported a "fine slice of truffle."

Perhaps what pleased her most was Escoffier's creation of *glace aux violettes,* her favorite flower. A half pound of violet petals was steeped for ten minutes in 1 1/2 pints of hot syrup. When strained and cooled, the juice of three lemons was added, and the recipe finished like any "common" water ice!

## CHAPTER 4

The *Larousse Gastronomique* lists Walnut Ketchup as an English condiment, which indeed it is. The recipe begins: "Put in a tub, with 2 or 3 pounds of rock salt, about 4 pounds of green walnut shells, mix well, and leave for 6 days, crushing the shells from time to time with a pestle. Leave the tub tilted to one side after each operation . . ."

Boiling, skimming, and the addition of ginger, cloves, and

cayenne follow, along with the admonition to wait several months before using.

Mushroom Ketchup is made in much the same way, in a "salting jar" with a sprinkling of pepper and allspice, and eventually pressed and boiled with thyme, bay, ginger, and marjoram.

As an "excellent sauce for eels," Dr. Kitchiner recommended a thick white sauce blended with Port, mushroom ketchup, and the vinegar from pickled onions. Isabella Beeton advised: "Choose full-grown mushroom-flaps, and take care they are perfectly *fresh-gathered* when the weather is tolerably dry."

And a contemporary recipe for Pickled Walnut Sauce (for cold shellfish) calls for "2 to 3 teaspoons mushroom ketchup."

For Oyster Ketchup, Mrs. Beeton suggests that one "procure the oysters very fresh, and open sufficient to fill a pint measure." A pint of sherry is added, with three ounces of salt, one "drachm" of cayenne, and two "drachms" of pounded mace. Then the whole thing is pounded "until reduced to a pulp," rubbed through a sieve, bottled, and corked "closely."

While still on the subject of ketchups, mention should be made of the one described in *The Experienced English House-Keeper* of 1778 that is promised to keep for seven years. "Take two quarts of the oldest strong beer you can get, put to it one quart of red wine, three quarters of a pound of anchovies . . ." This is boiled with shallots, mace, nutmegs, cloves, and three large "races" (roots) of ginger, "till one third is wasted; the next day bottle it for use; it may be carried to the East-Indies."

In her famous cookbook, *The Art of Cookery,* pioneering Mrs. Hannah Glasse gives instructions for a sauce for "Captains of Ships," and also the making of a ketchup "to be taken around the world."

Sauces continued to fascinate the British. No doubt the most enduring was Soyer's Reform, named for his club. Demi-glace and poivrade sauce are combined with a julienne of gherkins, smoked tongue, truffles, mushrooms, and the white of a hard-cooked egg. Lamb, or mutton, cutlets "Reform" indicate this elegant accompaniment. On a menu of the club, 9 *Mai,* 1846, *cotelettes de Mouton galloise à la Réforme* are featured.

Soyer also offered a "new and economical lobster sauce" made by simmering the pounded shell and soft parts, passing the liquid through a hair sieve, and adding melted butter, cayenne, and "a piece of anchovy butter the size of a walnut," any "red spawn," more fresh butter, and a little lemon juice. "An anchovy pounded with the shells of the lobster would be an improvement," he suggests.

A far less "economical" sauce is his *Financière,* whose very name suggests wealth. To begin: "Put a wineglassful of Sherry into a stew-pan with a piece of glaze the size of a walnut . . ." After the addition of "twelve fresh blanched mushrooms, twelve pre-pared cock's-combs, a throat sweetbread cut in thin slices, two French preserved truffles also in slices, and twelve small veal forcemeat quenelles . . ." Boil, skim, thin, and season "very palatably."

Francatelli may have been the first chef to use jelly in game sauces. His sauce for venison is based on melted currant jelly with red wine, sugar, lemon rind, cloves, and a cinnamon stick. Today Cumberland sauce is a frequent accompaniment to both wild and domestic meat.

Another, that he called "Neapolitan" for his homeland, con-tains, with the jelly and wine, a quantity of brown gravy and horseradish, which makes it sound a bit more English than Italian.

To celebrate Prince Albert's dream-come-true, a dessert was de-vised. Here is the "method" for "Crystal Palace Pudding." A plain mold is lined with lemon jelly decorated with fruit. Isinglass is dissolved in milk, and egg yolks, vanilla, and sugar are beaten in. When cool, this is poured into the lined mold, and when chilled and turned out, the whole dome is covered with "stiff liquid lemon jelly." Not exactly a Brunelleschi, but the glittering effect must have reminded many Britons of their industrial exhibition.

The following three, from Escoffier's directions, were favorites during the Savoy days.

*Oeufs de pluviers à la Muscovite* were plovers' eggs hard-cooked, shelled, and each one placed on a bed of caviar in a tiny tart shell just slightly larger than the egg.

*Cuisses de nymphes à l'aurore* were the famous frogs' legs poached in white wine, dipped in a pinkish-gold (dawn-colored) *chaud-froid* of fish *fumet* and paprika, and arranged on a layer of champagne aspic in a silver dish or crystal bowl. Chervil and tarragon leaves were laid around to simulate "water-grasses," and the whole was covered with more champagne, or Moselle, aspic to give an underwater impression.

The dish was brought to the table "set in a block of ice, fashioned as fancy may suggest."

*Coupe Adelina Patti* was vanilla ice cream served in footed sherbet glasses, with brandied cherries rolled in sugar placed around the edges so that their stems hung down and they could be "taken with a finger and thumb."

*Poires Belle Hélène* have rung many changes since Escoffier rechristened them *poires Hélène*. At Maxim's, where the Prince of Wales was pleased to be "known but not noticed," the peeled pears were cored from underneath, so that the stem remained, poached, and, when cool, filled with a sweet butter-cream of powdered almonds.

The pears were then set upright on a bed of vanilla ice cream, and chocolate sauce was poured over them, to coat them like their peel. The stems were ornamented with leaves of marzipan.

*"Pears Mona Lisa"* were whole fresh pears, peeled and poached in vanilla syrup, cooled, dried, and dipped into melted chocolate. Vanilla ice cream was then placed in tulip-shaped pastry shells, and a chocolate-coated pear set into the ice cream. The shells were presented in a gondola plate, decorated with fresh flowers.

Let us hope, as much for tradition as for sentiment, that some of those flowers were violets.

## CHAPTER 5

Auguste created *fraises Ritz* for César and his "little house" in Paris.

"Hull 1 lb. large strawberries and put into serving dish. Sprinkle with sugar and keep on ice until required. Rub 4 oz. wild strawberries and 4 oz. raspberries through a sieve and mix the purée with 1/2 pt. well-beaten Chantilly cream. When ready to serve cover the strawberries completely with the cream."

That is from *Ma Cuisine.* The earlier *Guide Culinaire* suggests the addition of "a little raspberry sauce to the purée, that it may acquire a pink tint."

*Caneton à la Rouenaisse* is a duckling stuffed with chopped onions, seasoned duck livers, and parsley, ground and run through a sieve. The bird is then roasted, underdone, in a very hot oven.

The duckling is cut into serving pieces, the breast sliced, the legs grilled, the stuffing removed, and the carcass sprinkled with brandy and lemon juice, and pressed. The juices from the press are added to a Rouenaisse sauce (Bordelaise with red wine and puréed Rouen duck livers, barely poached) and strained over the sliced breast.

*Oeufs Meyerbeer,* named for the composer of *Les Huguenots* and

*L'Africaine,* and the popular dish whose production Escoffier sim-
plified, demands that two eggs be fried, or baked in the oven,
*sur le plat,* with very hot butter, and served immediately with a
grilled lamb kidney in between, and around the edge a ring of
*Périgueux,* a rich Madeira sauce with chopped truffles. As is sometimes the case with artists, Meyerbeer's eggs are seen more often
than his operas.

An even more elegant egg dish of the day was *oeufs Jockey Club.*
Here the eggs were sautéed and trimmed with a cutter, so that
only a narrow rim of white remained. They were placed on croutons spread with a purée of foie gras; sometimes the purée was
also piped over the eggs.

   These were then arranged in a crown shape on a round platter,
with a slice of truffle on each egg, and in the center veal kidneys
sautéed with truffles in a Madeira demi-glace.

   Jules Gouffé, friend of Dumas and chef at the Jockey Club, also
contributed a recipe for foie gras steeped in cognac, studded with
truffles, sealed in butter, and wrapped in dough "shaped in the
form of a turnover."

   After being decorated and glazed, it was baked and served with
*sauce Madère,* reduced, and extra truffles!

The famous Jockey Club also had a famous salad, two versions of
which appear in Escoffier cookbooks. One describes equal quantities of asparagus tips and raw truffles in julienne, seasoned separately and then combined with a spicy mayonnaise.

   The second adds a julienne of chicken breasts to the asparagus
and truffles, and advises that the mayonnaise be thinned with an
oil-and-vinegar dressing.

Another popular salad of that time was the "Francillon," described in detail in the play of the same name by Alexandre
Dumas *fils,* who apparently inherited his father's interest in cui-

sine. The salad, also known as "Japanese," consists of potatoes cooked in broth, sliced, and seasoned while hot with salt, pepper, "a very good fruity olive oil," tarragon vinegar, white wine, and *fines herbes.*

The potatoes are mixed with large mussels, chilled, arranged in the shape of "a wise man's skull cap," and decorated with truffles cooked in champagne. Chrysanthemum blossoms are added in Japan.

Escoffier's version does not mix the mussels with the potatoes, but suggests an arrangement of mussels and truffles in alternate layers on top.

The "Francillon" salad also turns up in Denmark. There the mussels are boiled for ten minutes in just enough white wine to cover. The liquid is then cooked down, cooled, and mixed with mayonnaise and mustard to taste.

This dressing is poured over the mussels, which are covered next with sliced boiled potatoes, sprinkled with salt and pepper, and "an inkling of very finely minced parsley."

Dumas *père,* never at a loss, naturally had *his* favorite salad: "I place the yolk of one hard-boiled egg for each two persons in a salad-bowl. I moisten it with oil and crush it to make a paste of it. To this paste I add a little chervil, some minced tarragon, some ground anchovies, some chopped gherkins and the whites of hard-boiled eggs also chopped fine. Salt and pepper.

"Over it all I sprinkle a good vinegar, then I put the lettuce in the salad-bowl. At this point I summon a servant to toss the salad. When he has finished, I drop a pinch of paprika on it from a good height. It is now ready to be served."

Escoffier once said: "Of all the items in a menu, soup is that which exacts the most delicate perfection and the strictest attention, for on the first impression it gives to the diner, the success of the rest of the meal must depend."

For his good friend, Sarah Bernhardt, he created a soup of chicken consommé thickened with tapioca and poured over sliced quenelles of chicken forcemeat with crayfish butter, and slices of poached beef marrow. Also included were a julienne of "very black truffles" and the same amount of asparagus tips.

*Consommé favori de Sarah Bernhardt* is an essence of veal, herbs, and vegetables, puréed and mixed with an equal amount of tomato *velouté*, then served with vermicelli simmered in broth, drained, and tossed with butter and grated Parmesan.

The delicate *madeleines* which opened the door to Marcel Proust's remembrance of things past are said to have been invented by Talleyrand's pastry cook. Others say they are much older than that, having first appeared at Versailles in the court of Louis XV.

A recipe from Proust's time for "those short, plump little cakes called *'petites madeleines,'* which look as though they had been moulded in the fluted scallop of a pilgrim's shell," gives us the ingredients of butter, sugar, flour, eggs, brandy, salt, grated lemon peel, and baking soda, beaten together, poured to fill 2/3 of each *madeleine* mold, and baked until light tan.

## CHAPTER 6

Jugged hare is a very old dish that is still served in the jug-shaped earthenware pot it is cooked in. Small joints of hare are marinated in olive oil and brandy, browned, and then simmered in a good game stock that also includes an onion stuck with cloves, chopped bacon, a cut-up lemon, mushroom ketchup (!), a glass of dry red wine, and a bunch of sweet herbs, among other seasonings.

"Ali-Bab" in his *Encyclopedia of Practical Gastronomy* maintains that only an elderly rabbit need be marinated.

"Cover the jug close, that nothing may get in, and set it in a pot of boiling water and three hours will do it," wrote John Farley in 1783.

A sauce is made with the reduced stock, the hare's blood, its liver (if it is "quite sound," as Dr. Kitchiner cautions), currant jelly, and port.

The jug with hare and sauce comes to the table wrapped in a white napkin and accompanied by additional jelly, string beans, Brussels sprouts, puréed chestnuts, sautéed mushrooms, fried hominy, dry toast, dumplings, watercress, fresh dill, stewed prunes, and more red wine.

Trifles are old and famous British offerings: party desserts made in one's best crystal, cut-glass, or silver bowls. Sponge cake, ladyfingers, almond biscuits, or macaroons, or a combination of them all (slightly stale, with the ladyfingers poking up to make a border) are laid in the bottom of the bowl and moistened with sherry. Should the wine "not be found quite sufficient, add a little more, as the cakes should be well soaked," is Mrs. Beeton's sound advice.

Grated lemon rind and slivered almonds are sprinkled over, and then a coating of raspberry, strawberry, or apricot jam. Occasionally a second layer is made. Onto this is poured a rich custard, and when it has cooled and the dish is chilled, it is heaped with sweetened whipped cream, "which should stand as high as possible."

Over this may be laid strips of angelica and bands of currant jelly, strewn with glacéed fruit, crystallized violets and rose petals, and silver *dragées*.

Tipsy cakes, sometimes known in America as tipsy puddings or tipsy parsons, are close relatives of trifles. Usually only one kind of cake is used (mostly sponge), and brandy or Cognac accompany the sherry, along with almond essence. The custard is poured around and the whipped cream is served separately, since the surface is ornamented with a design of toasted almonds.

One recipe calls for forty ladyfingers in lieu of cake, another for a browned meringue icing; Mrs. Beeton prefers "decorating the top with cut preserved fruit."

As in all antique recipes, there are many variations and hand-me-downs of these. The ever-resourceful Italians have one they call *zuppa Inglese* (English soup). Three layers of cake are lightly drenched with rum, and spread with jam and custard. The fourth layer, the top, is inlaid with fresh or candied fruit, and the sides are thickly iced with whipped cream.

Two of the entrées created by Escoffier for the coronation of his old friend and new King were *poularde Edouard VII* and *selle d'agneau de lait Edouard VII*.

The pullet was stuffed with a pilaf of rice, foie gras, and truffles in the fashion of *poularde Derby.* Then it was poached without browning, and coated with a pale *sauce suprême* to which curry powder and diced pimientos were added. A garnish of sliced cucumbers in cream was served on the side.

The saddle, or rack, of baby lamb was boned with the skin left to appear untouched; then reshaped, filled out with a mixture of truffled and seasoned foie gras, marinated in Madeira. Poached in good stock until done, it was fitted into an oval terrine, from which the fat was skimmed before serving the lamb very cold.

Among the traditional treats of *Réveillon,* the supper after Christmas Eve midnight Mass, are *boudins,* those "black" blood puddings, said to be Assyrian in origin. The puddings, really sausages, are made from pork fat and blood, chopped onions, sometimes a few bread crumbs, and some cream, salt and pepper, nutmeg, fennel, and parsley.

Achille Ozanne, who wrote a poem about *boudins,* adds a glass of cognac.

The ingredients are stuffed into the pig's intestines, which are then cut and tied, poached and grilled. "White" puddings are made in the same way with lean pork meat and fat. Mashed potatoes and sautéed apples go with the sausages.

In French Canada, where the "puddings" are baked in pastry, they are called *tourtières,* for the name of the pie plate. But there are some who claim it is because the pork pies were marked to resemble turtles.

For the *"gros souper,"* Christmas Eve in Provence, snails and *aïoli* are customary.

Doubtless to many eyes, particularly young eyes, the star of any *Réveillon* is the *bûche de nöel,* the chocolate-frosted "yule-log" cake. The layer may be of sponge or chocolate and is baked on a jelly-roll sheet. It is spread with a butter cream (the Countess de Toulouse-Lautrec laced hers with Grand Marnier), rolled up, and coated with a chocolate icing flavored with coffee or rum.

The roll is cut at angles to resemble a log, and the frosting is applied roughly and scored with a fork for a bark-like effect. But it is in its decorations that this *gâteau* is most appealing.

Little toadstools made of marzipan or meringue and dotted with dry cocoa are stuck into the frosting; pistachio nuts are added to simulate moss. Spun-sugar moss is particularly beautiful. Powdered sugar and shredded coconut are sprinkled lightly over to resemble snow. And a wreath of red roses, mistletoe, or holly surrounds the platter.

*Langues-de-chat,* another child's delight, are crisp dry biscuits, narrow, flat, and thin as a cat's tongue. They are made with cake flour, egg whites, butter, sugar, and vanilla extract.

The batter is piped through a pastry tube into small strips on a baking sheet, and cooked until slightly browned. These are served with water ices in animal shapes.

There is also a delightful dessert called *mousse du chat,* made in a charlotte mold lined with "cat's tongues," filled with chocolate mousse, and served with coffee custard.

*Poulet Basquais* is a specialty of Biarritz which Edward certainly enjoyed. A roasting chicken, stuffed with a sprig of tarragon and a branch of thyme, is browned in goose fat. Then it is covered with warm broth and simmered with an onion, the peel of an orange, and *loukenkas,* highly spiced Basque sausage.

The bird is carved and presented on a bed of rice cooked in the stock, and surrounded by a sauce of sweet red peppers, tomatoes, herbs, and a piquant paprika-like seasoning called *piment Basquais.* The sausage is cut up and served over the chicken.

Easter is celebrated in Italy with a *torta pasqualina* (Easter pie). When Francatelli introduced his native dishes at Buckingham Palace, the royal family expressed pleasure. Traditionally this egg, cheese, and "spring greens" pie was made with dough divided into the number of years of Christ's life. The pastry is then rolled together to line a deep-dish pan. Chopped spinach, artichoke hearts, or other vegetables of the season are added and covered with Ricotta cheese.

Small wells are pressed into the filling to hold a dab of butter and a raw egg. Salt, pepper, marjoram, and Parmesan are sprinkled on, another layer of pastry covers the top, and the pie is baked until golden brown. It may be served hot or cold, and travels well to an Easter picnic.

A simpler version, and equally good, is one in which, quiche-like, a custard (and no top crust) covers the cheese and greens in the pastry shell. Sometimes hard-cooked quail, or bantam, eggs are included, eggs being one of the fertility symbols of the holiday. Now, with a bit of jugged hare . . .

"How times have changed!" crowed Carême. "Our great cooks in the old days used to serve *tourte* at the tables of princes . . . !" But times changed again, and in the days of King Edward VII *tourtes* were once again acceptable, especially at an Easter *fête champêtre.*

Other Edwardian hamper favorites, according to Lady Randolph Churchill, who should know, were cold lobster patties and quail puddings. The patties were made by mixing boiled chopped lobster meat with whipped cream, mayonnaise, tarragon, chervil, and aspic, and chilling until nearly set. Then a dash of tarragon vinegar, paprika, and cayenne is added, and the mixture is spooned gently into cream-puff pastry or patty shells.

For quail pudding, one quail per person is all that is allowed. The birds are marinated in oil and lemon juice, garlic and other herbs, then wrapped in paper-thin beef and placed with mushrooms, shallots, and parsley in a bowl lined with suet pastry. Stock is poured over; more pastry is spread on top, and the pudding is steamed over boiling water for an hour.

Finally, for a picnic incognito, what could be more suitable than Damson Fool? An old recipe calls for the boiling together of "3 dessertspoonfuls of brown sugar and 1/2 gill of water." 1 1/2 pints of damsons are added and cooked to a pulp.

This is sieved to remove stones and skins, and mixed with a pint of custard. When thick and cool, it is poured into small glasses and served with stiff cream.

## CHAPTER 7

So much has been written about *bouillabaisse* (a soup already called a legend), including poetry of sorts, that any further comment is purely self-indulgent. The word itself means to boil *(bouillir)* quickly over a fierce flame, and then lower *(baisser)*. And the word about its preparation is that to be authentic it should include the *rascasse, loup de mer, boudreuil, gurnet, fiélas, roucaou, saint-pierre, lophius,* and the conger eel, among others.

> One thing is sure . . . this fine Phocaean dish
> Is not the same without one master fish,
> The vulgar hogfish [*rascasse*], scorpion of the seas.
>                                          Joseph Méry

The bread served must be homemade *marette,* baked for the occasion, and the saffron in the soup should come from the autumn crocus that the Phoenicians grew along the banks of the sea.

This is probably sufficient to indicate that it is not only impossible but also unseemly to attempt to make this fish stew far from the port of Marseille. But there are alternate recipes in many American cookbooks, and (even though we may not have the seafood of the Mediterranean), olive oil, onions, garlic (called elsewhere in France "*la vanille de Marseille*"), parsley, orange peel, herbs, lean fish and shellfish, and French bread are fortunately available. Tomatoes came much later to the stewpot.

Because of the large variety of fish involved, this is a dish that should be served to a group of eight or ten. The hot stock is fused with the oil by rapid boiling, sprinkled with parsley, and poured over thick slices of heated bread rubbed with garlic. *Rouille,* a hot red pepper, garlic, and paprika sauce, may accompany it. The seafood is served separately, passed on a warm platter so that each guest may help himself.

> This *bouillabaisse* a noble dish is,
> A sort of soup, or broth, or brew.
>                                 W. M. Thackeray

Perhaps it depends on how hungry you are.

*Bagna cauda* is literally a "hot bath." Italian by origin, it comes from the Piedmont region near the French border, and its chief ingredients are those of Provence, too: olive oil, garlic, and anchovies. To make about a cup, melt a stick of butter with 1/4 cup of olive oil, stirring, not letting it boil or brown. Add six large cloves of garlic, minced; a two-ounce tin of flat anchovy filets, crushed; a few turns of freshly ground pepper and a miserly pinch of salt.

When this is smooth, keep it hot, and dip into it raw chilled vegetables: celery, carrot, and fennel sticks; cauliflower and broccoli flowerettes; strips of sweet red and green pepper and endive; unpeeled rounds of cucumber, cherry tomatoes, fresh mushrooms. Traditionally *grissini* (thin bread sticks) are also dipped in, and Barolo is poured.

Henri Charpentier, who colorfully described the episode in which he "invented" *crêpes Suzette* for the Prince of Wales, lists the ingredients of his sauce: four tablespoons of vanilla sugar, the juice and skins of two oranges, the juice and skin of one lemon, and 1/8 pound of butter. The peels are cut into julienne, and all is brought to a boil, adding one teaspoon of orange-blossom water, two ponies of kirsch, two ponies of white Curaçao, two ponies of rum, and one pony of maraschino.

While the pancakes are bubbling in this sauce, ponies of each of the cordials are blended and then flamed and poured over. For this, Henri received from the "world's most perfect gentleman" the gift of a ring, a Panama hat, and a cane.

A few years ago Jean Combet, chef at the Paris Ritz, revealed that "small quantities are the root of the matter. A very little butter on the dish, very small shavings of orange peel, a little Grand Marnier, a little caramel sauce, a little orange juice. When these and the dish are very hot, put on the pancake; after a moment, turn it (still flat), then add a *noisette* of fresh butter, a little sprinkle of sugar, a little lemon juice. Then fold the pancake over, add a little Cusenier *extra sec* orange liqueur, a touch more sugar, a little squeeze of lemon . . ."

Combet begins with a ready-made pancake, which he considers safe at a place like the Ritz, where quality is never in question. Escoffier, in his instructions, added: "When the pancake is intended for *crêpes Suzette,* it should be flavoured with curaçao and tangerine juice and coated with softened butter similarly flavoured."

*"Omelette Norvégienne,"* wrote André Simon, "is the name in the Cuisine Classique of the original *Omelette surprise,* that is, an ice-cream served inside a sweet Soufflé."

Escoffier, who amazed and delighted diners with his *bombe Nero,* directs for his "Norwegian Omelet" the laying of sliced sponge cake on a baking dish with a pyramid of ice cream and fruit spread with a meringue thick enough to brown on the outside in a hot oven without melting the inside.

Incidentally, these *omelettes surprises,* Baked Alaskas, or whatever they may be called, no longer pose as "surprises." Some gourmets even suggest that the best aspect of these particular desserts is the anticipation of them!

Once, during his Savoy years, Escoffier received a request from a "very important lady" to instruct her cook in the making of omelets. Upon arriving at the house, Auguste found that there was no *poêle,* the French omelet pan of the sort he had brought to Britain in his suitcase, although "she was nevertheless a very famous English cook."

Being Escoffier, he returned the next day with a *poêle,* and all were content.

The Dauphiné region of France is famous for its potatoes, as well as for other good things. *Gratin de pommes de terre à la Dauphinoise* is a dish of thinly sliced potatoes mixed with scalded milk, a beaten egg, freshly grated Gruyère, salt and pepper, and a grind or two of nutmeg. This is poured into a buttered earthenware baking dish rubbed with a clove of garlic; the potato mixture is sprinkled well with more Gruyère and a few *noisettes* of butter, and baked for about an hour in a moderate oven.

For *pommes de terre à la Savoyarde,* hot white stock or consommé replaces the milk. Some traditionalists suggest that the cheese should appear only in the *Savoyarde* potatoes, with the *Dauphinoise* being simply potatoes and cream. Others suggest a mingling of Parmesan with the Gruyère. In any case, the top should be glossy and brown, and the whole served very hot in its earthenware dish.

Gioacchino Antonio Rossini is perhaps best known for his *Barber of Seville,* but his name has also been associated with many culinary creations, most of them extravagant, most of them delicious, and most employing the foie gras-truffle-Madeira sauce triumvirate that became his trademark.

Some he invented himself, including a sweet omelet that bears no part of the trademark. Others were invented years after his death in 1868. Escoffier named another omelet for him, and this one is easy to identify, with its eggs beaten with foie gras and diced truffles, and served with additional foie gras and truffles and a demi-glace of truffle essence all around.

*Escalopes de ris de veau Rossini* adds pasta as a tribute to the Italian. Sweetbreads are blanched, sliced, and arranged in a ring. A piece of sautéed foie gras is laid on each slice, and a truffled Madeira sauce is poured over all. The center is filled with noodles tossed with Parmesan and butter.

By far the most famous Rossini dish is the *tournedos.* One story of its creation is that on a certain evening in the Café Anglais the composer declared the beef filet he was eating to be tasteless and demanded his favorite garniture. When the maître d'hôtel protested that this would be unpresentable, Rossini is reported to have said: "Then serve it behind my back." Thus the word *"tourne le dos"* (turn the back), or so the story goes.

There are some who insist that Escoffier invented *tournedos Rossini.* His recipe describes sautéeing the filets in butter and setting them on croutons of the same size, also sautéed in butter and spread with meat jelly. Each *tournedos* is topped with a crown of seasoned foie gras, and over that is set "a fine slice of truffle."

The sauce is the Madeira demi-glace with truffles; and a dish of hot noodles with butter and Parmesan is served separately. Nothing is said about back-turning.

From *Le Guide Culinaire,* here is what is perhaps Escoffier's most famous sauce, *Diable.* Two ounces of sliced shallots and 1/3 pint of white wine are combined in a saucepan and reduced to 2/3; 1/2 pint of demi-glace is added, and the mixture is reduced to 2/3 again. It is seasoned strongly with cayenne, and strained through muslin. Besides being an accompaniment to grilled fowls or pigeons, it may also be served with "left-over meat which needs a spicy sauce."

Carême, La Reynière, Brillat-Savarin, and others of their times and inclinations might have been disturbed by the mention of leftover meat, but the Little Sisters of the Poor would have understood and bestowed their blessing.

# BIBLIOGRAPHY

This is in no sense a definitive list of books about Escoffier, his period, his cuisine, or about cooking in general. It is simply intended to indicate what I found of value in my particular approach. And I also found no statement ever truer than that one good book leads to another.

## COOKBOOKS

I *Italian*

Boni, Ada. *Italian Regional Cooking.* New York: E. P. Dutton, 1969.

Carnacina, Luigi. *Great Italian Cooking.* New York: Abradale Press, 1968.

delle Cinqueterre, Berengario. *The Renaissance Cookbook.* Crown Point, Ind.: Dunes Press, 1975.

Hazen, Marcella. *The Classic Italian Cook Book.* New York: Harper and Row, 1973.

II *French*

Black, Colette. *The French Provincial Cookbook.* New York: Crowell-Collier, 1963.

Charpentier, Henri. *The Henri Charpentier Cookbook.* Los Angeles: Price/Stern/Sloan, 1970.

Claiborne, Craig, and Pierre Franey. *Classic French Cooking.* New York: Time-Life Books, 1970.

Courtine, Robert. *The Hundred Glories of French Cooking.* New York: Farrar, Straus & Giroux, 1973.

Curnonsky (Sailland). *Les Recettes de Philomene.* Paris: Guy le Prat, 1949.

David, Elizabeth. *French Country Cooking.* London: John Lehmann, 1951.

———— *French Provincial Cooking.* New York: Harper and Row, 1962.

Donon, Joseph. *The Classic French Cuisine.* New York: Alfred A. Knopf, 1959.

Escoffier, Auguste. *Le Guide Culinaire.* Paris: Ernest Flammarion & Cie., 1903; New York: Crown Publishers, 1941.

———— *Ma Cuisine.* Paris: Ernest Flammarion & Cie., 1934; London: Paul Hamlyn, 1965.

Fisher, M. F. K. *The Cooking of Provincial France.* New York: Time-Life Books, 1968.

Kirschman, Irena. *French Cooking.* New York: Galahad Books, 1973.

Oliver, Raymond. *La Cuisine.* New York: Tudor Publishing, 1969.

Pasquet, Ernest. *La Patisserie Familiale.* Paris: Ernest Flammarion & Cie., 1958.

Pellaprat, Henri-Paul. *L'Art Culinaire Moderne.* Castagnola, Swisse: Jacques Kramer, 1956.

Point, Fernand. *Ma Gastronomie.* Connecticut: Lyceum Books, 1974.

Saint-Ange, Mme E. *La Bonne Cuisine.* Paris: Librarie Larousse, 1929.

Tanty, Francois. *La Cuisine Française.* Chicago: Inter-Ocean, 1894.

Toulouse-Lautrec, Henri, and Maurice Joyant. *The Art of Cuisine.* New York: Holt, Rinehart & Winston, 1966.

Toulouse-Lautrec, Comtesse de. *La Cuisine de France.* New York: The Orion Press, 1964.

III *British*

Beeton, Isabella. *The Book of Household Management.* New York: Farrar, Straus & Giroux, 1969.

Dutton, Joan Parry. *The Good Fare and Cheer of Old England.* New York: Reynal, 1960.

Heath, Ambrose. *The Queen Cookery.* London: Weidenfeld & Nicolson, 1960.

McKee, Mrs. *Royal Cookery Book.* London: Arlington Books, 1964.

Maclean, Lady Veronica. *Lady Maclean's Cook Book.* London: Collins, 1965.

Sass, Lorna J. *To the King's Taste.* New York: The Metropolitan Museum of Art, 1975.

Spry, Constance. *Come into the Garden, Cook.* London: J. M. Dent and Sons, 1952.

White, Florence. *Good Things in England.* London: Jonathan Cape, 1932.

IV *General*

Bang, Asta, and Edith Rode. *An Introduction to Danish Culinary Art.* Copenhagen: Jul. Gjellerups Forlag, 1955.

Carrier, Robert. *Great Dishes of the World.* New York: Random House, 1964.

Chamberlain, Narcissa G. *A Vintage Food Sampler.* New York: Vintage Books, 1962.

Claiborne, Craig. *An Herb and Spice Cook Book.* New York: Harper and Row, 1963.

Clair, Colin. *Of Herbs and Spices.* London: Abelard-Schuman, 1961.

Congressional Club. *Congressional Club Cook Book.* Washington, D.C.: 1970.

David, Elizabeth. *Mediterranean Food.* London: John Lehmann, 1950.

de Groot, Roy Andries. *Feasts for All Seasons.* New York: Alfred A. Knopf, 1966.

Gray, Peter. *The Mistress Cook.* New York: Oxford University Press, 1956.

Humphrey, Sylvia Windle. *A Matter of Taste.* New York: Macmillan, 1965.

Layton, T. A. *Cheese and Cheese Cookery.* New York: Crown Publishers, 1967.

MacNicol, Mary. *Flower Cookery.* New York: Collier Books, 1972.

Marquis, Vivienne, and Patricia Haskell. *The Cheese Book.* New York: Simon and Schuster, 1965.

Rosengarten, Frederic, Jr. *The Book of Spices.* New York: Pyramid Books, 1973.

Simon, André L. *The Wine and Food Menu Book.* London: Frederick Muller Ltd., n.d.

Tracy, Marion. *The Art of Making Real Soups.* New York: Doubleday, 1967.

## SPEAKING OF FOOD

Aresty, Esther B. *The Delectable Past.* New York: Simon and Schuster, 1964.

Bailey, Adrian. *The Cooking of the British Isles.* New York: Time-Life Books, 1969.

Beard, James. *Beard on Food.* New York: Alfred A. Knopf, 1974.

Brillat-Savarin, Jean Anthelme. *The Physiology of Taste.* New York: Doubleday, Page, 1926.

Chamberlain, Narcissa G. *The Flavor of Italy.* New York: Hastings House, 1965.

Chamberlain, Samuel. *Bouquet de France.* New York: Gourmet, 1966

———— British Bouquet. New York: Gourmet, 1963

———— Italian Bouquet. New York: Gourmet, 1963

Costa, Margaret. *London at Table.* New York: Gourmet, 1971.

Fisher, M. F. K. *The Art of Eating.* New York: Macmillan, 1954.
_____ *With Bold Knife and Fork.* New York: G. P. Putnam's Sons, 1969.
Fitzgibbon, Theodora. *A Taste of London.* Boston: Houghton Mifflin, 1975.
Furnas, C. C. and S. M. *Man, Bread and Destiny.* New York: Reynal & Hitchcock, 1937.
Guy, Christian. *An Illustrated History of French Cuisine.* New York: The Orion Press, 1962.
Herman, Judith and Marguerite Shalett. *The Cornucopia.* New York: Harper and Row, 1973.
Luke, Sir Harry. *The Tenth Muse.* London: Putnam, 1962.
McKendry, Maxime. *The Seven Centuries Cookbook.* New York: McGraw-Hill, 1973.
Masson, Lucia. *La Belle France.* London: Paul Hamlyn, 1964.
Norman, Barbara. *Tales of the Table.* Englewood Cliffs, N.J.: Prentice-Hall, 1972.
Papashvily, Helen and George. *Russian Cooking.* New York: Time-Life Books, 1969.
Root, Waverley. *The Cooking of Italy.* New York: Time-Life Books, 1968.
_____ *The Food of France.* New York: Alfred A. Knopf, 1958.
_____ *The Food of Italy.* New York: Atheneum, 1971.
Seranne, Ann, and John Tebbel. *The Epicure's Companion.* New York: David McKay, 1962.
Tannahill, Reay. *Food in History.* New York: Stein and Day, 1973.
Toulouse-Lautrec, Comtesse de. *Chez Maxim's.* New York: McGraw-Hill, 1962.
Trager, James. *The Foodbook.* New York: Grossman, 1970.
Wechsberg, Joseph. *Blue Trout and Black Truffles.* New York: Alfred A. Knopf, 1966.
Wolfe, Linda. *The Literary Gourmet.* New York: Random House, 1962.

## CULINARY REFERENCE

Babinsky, Henri ("Ali-Bab"). *Encyclopedia of Practical Gastronomy.* New York: McGraw-Hill, 1974.
Dumas, Alexandre. *Dictionary of Cuisine.* New York: Avon Books, 1958.
Lichine, Alexis. *Encyclopedia of Wines and Spirits.* New York: Alfred A. Knopf, 1969.
Montagné, Prosper. *Larousse Gastronomique.* New York: Crown Publishers, 1961.
Simon, André L. *Dictionary of Gastronomy.* New York: McGraw-Hill, 1970.
_____. *Wines of the World.* New York: McGraw-Hill, 1967.
Ward, Artemus. *The Encyclopedia of Food.* New York: Baker & Taylor, 1929.

## HISTORY

Aronson, Theo. *The Golden Bees:* The Story of the Bonapartes. Greenwich, Conn.: New York Graphic Society, 1964.
Barzini, Luigi. *The Italians.* New York: Atheneum, 1964.
Churchill, Winston S. *The Island Race.* London: Cassell, 1968.
de Gramont, Sanche. *The French.* New York: G. P. Putnam's Sons, 1969.
Durant, Will. *The Renaissance.* New York: Simon and Schuster, 1953.
_____ *The Reformation.* New York: Simon and Schuster, 1957.
Durant, Will and Ariel. *Rousseau and Revolution.* New York: Simon and Schuster, 1963.
Horne, Alistair. *The Fall of Paris.* New York: St. Martin's Press, 1965.
Maurois, André. *A History of France.* London: Jonathan Cape, 1949.
Petrie, Sir Charles. *The Edwardians.* New York: W. W. Norton, 1965.
Schevill, Ferdinand. *The Medici.* New York: Harcourt, Brace, 1949.

Stacton, David. *The Bonapartes.* New York: Simon and Schuster, 1966.

## BIOGRAPHY

Battiscombe, Georgina. *Queen Alexandra.* Boston: Houghton Mifflin, 1969.
Gathborne-Hardy, Robert, ed. *Memoirs of Lady Ottoline Morrell.* New York: Alfred A. Knopf, 1964.
Herbodeau, Eugene, and Paul Thalamas. *Georges Auguste Escoffier.* London: Practical Press, 1955.
Hetherington, John. *Melba.* New York: Farrar, Straus & Giroux, 1967.
Leslie, Anita. *Jennie:* The Life of Lady Randolph Churchill. New York: Charles Scribner's Sons, 1969.
Mack, Gerstle. *Toulouse-Lautrec.* New York: Alfred A. Knopf, 1953.
Maurois, André. *Lélia:* The Life of George Sand. New York: Harper and Brothers, 1954.
Morris, Helen. *Portrait of a Chef:* the Life of Alexis Soyer. London: Cambridge University Press, 1938.
Ritz, Marie Louise. *César Ritz,* Host to the World. Philadelphia: J. B. Lippincott, 1938.
Skinner, Cornelia Otis. *Madame Sarah.* Boston: Houghton Mifflin, 1967.
Van Dyke, Paul. *Catherine de Médicis.* New York: Charles Scribner's Sons, 1922.
Woodham-Smith, Cecil. *Queen Victoria.* New York: Alfred A. Knopf, 1972.
Young, G. F. *The Medici.* New York: Modern Library, 1930.

## THE SOCIAL SCENE

Allen, Reginald. *The First Night Gilbert and Sullivan.* New York: The Heritage Press, 1958.
Bennett, Arnold. *Imperial Palace.* New York: Doubleday, Doran, 1930.

Burton, Elizabeth. *The Pageant of Early Victorian England.* New York: Charles Scribner's Sons, 1972.

Frischauer, Willi. *The Grand Hotels of Europe.* New York: Coward-McCann, 1965.

Frizell, Bernard. *Escoffier,* God of the Gastronomes. New York: Horizon, 1961.

Higginbottom, David. *The Royal Pavilion, Brighton.* London: Lund Humphries, n.d.

Jackson, Stanley. *The Savoy:* The Romance of a Great Hotel. New York: E. P. Dutton, 1964.

Keppel, Sonia. *Edwardian Daughter.* London: Hamish Hamilton, 1958.

Laver, James. *Manners and Morals in the Age of Optimism, 1848–1914.* New York: Harper and Row, 1966.

Leslie, Anita. *The Marlborough House Set.* New York: Doubleday, 1973.

Lindsay, Jack. *The Complete Works of Gaius Petronius.* New York: Rarity Press, 1932.

Maurois, André. *The Edwardian Era.* New York: D. Appleton-Century, 1933.

Minney, R. J. *The Edwardian Age.* Boston: Little, Brown, 1964.

More, Jasper. *The Land of Italy.* London: B. T. Batsford, 1949.

Priestley, J. B. *Victoria's Heyday.* New York: Harper and Row, 1972.

Rouff, Marcel. *The Passionate Epicure.* New York: E. P. Dutton, 1962.

Roumagnac, Roger. *La France.* Paris: Odé, n.d.

Sackville-West, V. *The Edwardians.* New York: Doubleday, Doran, 1930.

Scott, J. M. *Vineyards of France.* London: Hodder & Stoughton, 1950.

Watts, Stephen. *The Ritz.* London: The Bodley Head, 1963.

Weintraub, Stanley. *The Savoy,* Nineties Experiment. University Park, Pa.: Pennsylvania State University Press, 1966.

# INDEX

DATE DUE